IMAGES
of America

BROOKLINE

Brookline Village, seen here from Parker Hill, *c.* 1840, was known as Punch Bowl Village, named after the tavern that stood in the Village Square area until 1833. (BPL.)

IMAGES
of America

BROOKLINE

Greer Hardwicke and Roger Reed

ARCADIA

First printed in 1998.
Reprinted in 2002.

Published by Arcadia Publishing,
an imprint of Tempus Publishing, Inc.
2A Cumberland Street
Charleston, SC 29401

Printed in Great Britain.

Library of Congress Catalog Card Number: 98-88058

For all general information contact Arcadia Publishing at:
Telephone 843-853-2070
Fax 843-853-0044
E-Mail sales@arcadiapublishing.com

For customer service and orders:
Toll-Free 1-888-313-2665

Visit us on the internet at http://www.arcadiapublishing.com

The town seal was adopted on April 3, 1848. The design represents agricultural and farming tools, reflecting Brookline's early heritage and a view of the city of Boston with a train running between the two. Brookline was initially known as Boston Cornfield and Boston Plantation. Francis N. Mitchell designed the seal. (BPC.)

CONTENTS

ACKNOWLEDGMENTS

The authors would like to thank the following for their invaluable assistance in this project. For financial support we would like to thank: the Friends of the Brookline Preservation Commission, the Brookline Chamber of Commerce, the Rotary Club of Brookline, Chobee Hoy Associates Real Estate, Hammond Residential Real Estate, Hunneman and Company/Coldwell Banker, and Chestnut Hill Realty. For their generous sharing of photographs, we thank the following people and institutions: the Brookline Public Library (BPL); the Society for the Preservation of New England Antiquities (SPNEA); the Brookline Preservation Commission (BPC); the National Park Service, Frederick Law Olmsted Site, the Longyear Museum and Society; the Francis Ouimet Society; the Museum of Transportation; the Rivers School; the Park School; John F. Kennedy Library; the Massachusetts Historical Society; the Library of Congress; Congregation Kehillath Israel; Shepley, Bulfinch, Richardson & Abbott; John J. Burns Library, Boston College; the Boston Gas Company; Aly and Jenna Kidrin; Earle G. Shettleworth Jr.; Dan Miranda; Joel Shield; Tim Sullivan; Hall Silloway; Eleanor Motley Richardson; Caroline Oveson Lovelace; and Lynn Osborn. We are also indebted to many people who assisted and encouraged us along the way: Ruth Dorfman, David England, Nancy Peabody, Irvin Taube, Samuel Shaw, Carla Wyman Benka, the Town of Brookline, Charles Bahne, the Brookline Engineering Department, the Brookline Preservation Commission, Dave Mansey, Glen Poré, Cheryl Moneyhun, John B. Atteberry, Mary Everett, Amy Schectman, Rachel Gackenheimer, Tom Condon, the staff of the Brookline Public Library (especially Ann Clark), Joyce Connolly, Lorna Condon, Mary Everett at the Rivers School, Cheryl Honeymeyer, Bob Donovan, Stephen Jerome, Steve Pendery, Amy Sutton, and the Wilson and Reed families.

One

THE TOWN GREEN

Brookline was known as the "Muddy River" or the "Muddy River Hamlet" for the first 75 years after Boston was settled. Initial settlers were inhabitants of Boston who kept their livestock there in the summer. The Town of Boston made over one hundred land grants between 1635 and 1642. In 1686, limited independence allowed residents to build a school and be exempt from Boston taxes, though they still had to worship at the meetinghouse in Roxbury. After several attempts, a petition to be a separate town, signed by 32 freeholders, was granted; Muddy River was incorporated as the Town of Brookline in 1705.

The Town Green area, lying at the intersection of Warren and Walnut Streets, was the geographic and demographic center of the town in 1697 when the first schoolhouse was built. It stood on the open space across from the Town Green. The Town Green was bisected by part of the old Sherburne Road, now Walnut Street, which was laid out in 1658 by the Massachusetts Bay Colony, probably along an old Native American trail. This road was the only land route west from Boston until the construction of the Worcester Turnpike in 1807.

When Brookline became independent in 1705, the important municipal structures were constructed near the center. In 1714-18, building of the first meetinghouse began near the schoolhouse, approximately where the First Parish stands on Walnut Street. Reverend James Allen was the first minister. A garrison house built on land bought from Samuel Clark was actually a log house with one door and no windows in the lower story. It was used as a fort with a storehouse for the entire town, in case of alarm from the Native Americans. The Old Burying Ground with a wooden fence around it was established in 1717, also on Clark's land. It originally had a New Lane (now Cypress to Washington Street) that was laid out in 1719 for residents in the northern section to attend town meetings; Woodward's Lane, now the southern part of Warren, was put in for the residents of the south section. From the triangular Town Green, three militia groups, alerted by William Dawes, set out to engage the British in July 1775. Later, two other meetinghouses were built; the rectory at 353 Walnut Street was built in 1856 when the earlier structure was destroyed by fire.

In 1844, a new town hall was built on Washington Street and the civic center moved there. The area around the Town Green, after the governmental shift to Brookline Village, settled into a residential enclave, much as it is today. A group of mid-19th-century houses were built along Chestnut Street, Chestnut Place, Walnut Street, Dudley Street, and Fairmont Street. A second wave of development around the turn of the century brought Colonial Revival, Queen Anne, and Shingle-Style houses, several of which replaced older Colonial and 19th-century structures. New streets were laid out including Welch and Hedge Roads, and Kennard Street. In the mid-20th century, the old 1715 Clark House was demolished and Clark Court was built. The Town Green is listed on the National Register of Historic Places.

The second meetinghouse was designed by architect Peter Banner and built on a new lot across the street from the old one. The cornerstone was laid on April 11, 1805. Contributed items included a bell, a Bible, and a baptismal font. The dedication was held on June 11, 1806. The new building was 68 by 64 feet and the 11-by-11-foot porch in front had lobbies on either side. (BPL.)

A view looking down Walnut Street toward Town Green in the 1880s shows a view of the 1856 rectory on the right, the 1824 town hall on the left, and the third meetinghouse, designed in 1848 by Brookline resident Edward C. Cabot, in the center. This Gothic Revival structure stood until 1891. It was replaced by the Romanesque church designed by Shepley, Rutan & Coolidge. (BPL.)

The Gardner-Sumner house at Warren and Walnut was built in 1740 by Nathaniel Gardner, a Boston merchant. Henry Hulton, a royal commissioner of customs bought it for a summer retreat and often entertained British soldiers at his house during the early years of the Revolutionary War. His house was later confiscated and sold. Architect Thomas W. Sumner and his wife, Elizabeth, bought the property in 1816, living there until his death in 1849. After Nathaniel Chapin owned it, the house was torn down in 1885 to make way for the Queen Anne house for Moses Williams. (SPNEA.)

Reverend John Pierce, pastor of First Parish from 1796 to 1849, was the church's fifth minister, also serving as chair of the school committee for over 50 years. According to Harriet Woods, in *Historical Sketches*, Pierce was a man of "magnetic vitality, great powers of spiritual leadership, and an effective cultural influence in the community." His 53-year tenure ended at his death in 1849. The town later named the primary and grammar schools in Brookline Village after him. (BPL.)

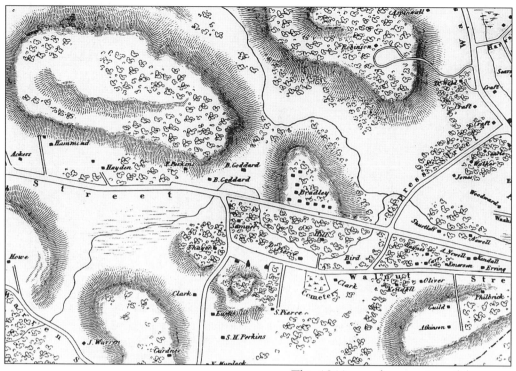

This 1844 map shows a view of the Town Green area at the end of Walnut Street. The cemetery is shown, as is the parish house (labeled Pierce), the Sumner House, and the Thayer property, a portion of which would become the Brookline Reservoir. The schoolhouse and the meetinghouse are at the corner of Walnut and Warren Streets. Also on the map are the Bird estate and the Hill-Ogden-Kennard House. (BPC.)

In 1824, the town voted to build a two-story building for a schoolhouse and town house designed by Thomas W. Sumner. Dedicated on January 1, 1825, it has been the site of schools, town meetings, religious services, temperance lectures, Lyceum lectures, and several singing schools. In 1890, the First Parish Church bought it and renamed it Pierce Hall, after Reverend John Pierce. In 1906, the church, both literally and architecturally, incorporated it into the body of the church. Note the sheds for riding carriages and horses in this 1875 view. (BPL.)

This view was taken around 1888 of the Hill-Kennard-Ogden House, known as "The Maples." Designed by Gridley F. Bryant in 1843–44, it was the country house for Jeremiah Hill, a Boston commission merchant. It was sold by the family in 1869 to Martin Perry Kennard, a jeweler, customs house collector, and U.S. sub-treasurer. The large estate was subdivided in 1897 when Kennard and Hedge Roads were laid out and houses were constructed. (BPL.)

A 1950s view shows the same property when it was the Park School. The Park School was started by Caroline Pierce in 1888; Julia Park took it over in 1910, renaming it in 1913. In 1927, the school moved here, using the house, barn-turned-gym, and several buildings on Hedge Road. The town bought it in the late 1960s when the Park School moved and became part of the Lincoln School. (Courtesy Park School.)

Pictured is a late 19th-century Memorial Day celebration at the Old Burying Ground, established in 1717, on Walnut Street. The land was purchased from Samuel Clark Jr., the Clark family homestead having been built nearby in 1715. The cemetery is on the site of an old garrison house. In 1840, the town built a stone wall around the grounds and the entrance moved to the present location. It was the only town cemetery until 1875 when Walnut Hills was established in an undeveloped site off Allandale Road. (BPL.)

Harvey and Kate Crowell Cushing moved to Brookline in 1912, buying the old Bird estate at 305 Walnut Street. It was a yellow house with a white picket fence and a tennis court. Dr. Cushing was an early neurosurgeon known for his description of Cushing's disease and a Pulitzer Prize winning book on the life of Sir. Dr. William Osler (1925). He had come to Boston to spearhead the new Peter Bent Brigham Hospital. In 1942, the property was torn down and developed by Goldie Sklaver, a Brookline developer. (BPL.)

The gatehouse for the Brookline Reservoir, designed by Charles E. Parker *c.* 1847, is a classical building with a closed pediment and quoins. In 1902, the City of Boston decided to sell the reservoir and its surrounding land. Prompted by rumors of undesired development, the neighbors, including Amy Lowell, John C. Olmsted, Walter Channing, Edward Atkinson, and George Lee, contributed more than $50,000 towards the land's purchase price of $150,000. In 1926, the gatehouse was altered to provide rooms and toilet facilities for swim meets, skating, and other occasions. (BPL.)

The reservoir is a man-made body of water approximately 1 mile around. In Revolutionary times, the land, then a pasture with a marsh and a stream, belonged to the Gardner family. In 1800, Richard Sullivan bought it and built a large house on the land near Sherburne Road. Eventually 30 acres were purchased for $58,419 to become part of the Cochituate water system that fed into the Beacon Hill Reservoir. On October 14, 1848 at 2 p.m., the first water from Lake Cochituate arrived at a fountain on the Boston Common. (BPL.)

A view of Walnut Street looks from the Brookline Reservoir towards the Town Green. In the 1880s, Alice Bowditch obtained the property. In 1896, her nephew Ernest Bowditch, the landscape architect, bought it for subdivision. Bowditch himself hired Hartwell, Richardson & Driver to design the house on the right. Its earliest tenants were the daughters of John Boyle O'Reilly, editor of *The Boston Pilot*. The Colonial Revival on the left was designed by Julius Schweinfurth for Frederick Coffin in 1898. In the rear is a Colonial Revival house built by architect Joseph E. Chandler. (BPL.)

Two

BROOKLINE VILLAGE

Brookline Village became the civic and commercial center after the erection of the second town house in 1844 and the arrival of the railroad in 1847. The original development centered on land allotments around lower Washington Street after the building of a cart bridge over the Muddy River in 1639. Various roads were laid: a road to Sherburne (1658); Harvard Street, the road to the colleges (1662); and the Newtown Road to Watertown, now Washington (1657). In 1650, 25 families lived near the bridge. By 1806, most activity in this area centered around the Punch Bowl Tavern, erected near Pearl Street about 1730. In 1806, a stagecoach route was inaugurated, along with the beginning of construction for the Boston and Worcester Turnpike (now Route 9).

Before the 1840s, this area had been pastoral with scattered houses. Along the Muddy River were marshes and a tidal gate; oyster beds even existed here for a time. Auxiliary streets were usually cart roads, such as Kent Street (originally Harrison Place), or paths to homesteads, such as Perry's Lane. The village brook running along the railroad tracks wasn't covered until the late 19th century. The new town house and the railroad accelerated residential and commercial development. Whole sections radiating from the main roads were developed, such as White Place and the Linden area. This period also saw the settling of Irish and German immigrants who came out from Boston. Blacksmiths, livery stables, and carpenter and paint shops emerged in the 1850s and 1860s around Pearl and Boylston Streets. Several gasometers were built by the Brookline Gas Company. Before the Civil War, most commercial activity took place below the bridge.

After the war, panel brick buildings replaced wooden ones and the commercial area expanded up Washington and Harvard Streets. A new town hall was erected in the 1870s, and two new fire stations were built along with a myriad of houses along Cypress, Kent, Brook, Aspinwall, Perry, Francis, Davis, and Gorham Streets. A wealth of Stick Style, Queen Anne, Colonial Revival, and Shingle Style double- and single-family houses filled out the remaining empty land. Worker housing and triple-deckers stood along Boylston, Pearl, and Emerald Streets. The Congregational, Baptist, Presbyterian, and Catholic churches were built. The Muddy River was transformed into an urban park by Frederick Law Olmsted in the 1880s.

The modest housing and commercial buildings along lower Washington Street fell victim to urban redevelopment in the 1960s, being replaced by office buildings. The train line became the Highland branch of the Metropolitan Transit Authority. However, the 1970s brought a renewed interest in the 19th-century Brookline Village and the town, citizens, and businesses began to restore the houses and storefronts.

Aspinwall Avenue in the 1880s included the Peter Aspinwall house and St. Paul's Church. Peter Aspinwall bought a farm in the Muddy River in 1650. This First Period House was built a decade later. The large elm was planted by Samuel Aspinwall, c. 1700. The house was torn down in 1891, and today is the site of the Ward playground. St. Paul's Church, the first Episcopal church in Brookline, was designed by Richard Upjohn, dedicated in 1852. (Courtesy Jenna and Aly Kidrin.)

This Gothic Revival house, built at a cost off $5,000, still stands on Washington Street. Richard Bond designed it for the widow of Captain John Candler when she came to Brookline around 1850. Her two sons, John L. and William, became merchants. John L. Candler later served as a state representative and as a U.S. Congressman. The picturesque view with the pond shows the sylvan nature of Brookline at mid-century. The pond was filled in by 1900. (Published in *American Cottage and Villa Architecture*, 1850. Courtesy SPNEA.)

The Benjamin Davis house, at the corner of Washington and Davis, was built *c.* 1760, and represents the first phase of development in the village. Davis Avenue was known as Washington Place. The Davis family were early settlers and very involved in town affairs. The homestead was torn down in 1867 and replaced by the St. Andrew's building in 1875 by John Panter. (BPL.)

This Gothic Revival house was built by Elijah Emerson in 1846. Emerson, a director of the Second National Bank and president of the Middlesex Horse Railroad, bought a portion of the Davis family's land. At one time, the Emerson estate had a small pond with a gazebo. During the 1880s, he began to develop his land, erecting ten houses for rent. In 1907, after Emerson's death, his two daughters sold 2 acres to the town for a park, which was named Emerson Garden. The house and barn were then relocated across the street on Davis Avenue. (BPL.)

This house overlooking Linden Park was built by Thomas Aspinwall Davis, a jeweler and once mayor of Boston (1844). Davis was one of the first to develop his family's farm into a planned community. It was laid out as a "garden suburb" and was restricted to residences; manufacturing was not allowed. Boston merchants quickly populated the Linden area, designed in 1843–44 by Alexander Wadsworth and John F. Edwards. Davis's house was moved around the corner in 1906. (BPL.)

A view of the garden of the Charles B. Dana house, built c. 1861 on Harvard Avenue, looks at the spire of the Congregational church fronting School Street. The church was built in 1844 and the congregation moved to its present location at Harvard and Marion Streets in 1873. The Dana house shows the rural nature of the village in the mid-19th century. (BPL.)

This Italianate was the Edward C. Wilson house and carriage barn, 1855, which stood on Harvard Street, near Alton Place, where there is now a Stop&Shop. Brookline Village and Coolidge Corner were developed in the mid-19th century, after Beacon Street and the train arrived, and included grand estates and modest houses such as those on Vernon and Auburn Streets. The Wilson house was demolished in 1924 to make way for the new rage of the era, the automobile and its garage. (BPL.)

This photograph shows the first floor of the Seaman's building at the corner of Davis and Washington Streets. It replaced an 1845 store on the Seth Thayer estate. The earlier building had a second-story hall, which was used by dancing schools and singing schools. It was also used for a clubroom and political gatherings. In 1912, W.D. Paine, a stationer, replaced the Seaman's family business, moving from 239 Washington. Commercial and residential units remain today. (BPC.)

Here is a view of Harvard Square in Brookline Village, *c.* 1895. Next to it was the Lowe Building, built 1892. Harvard Hall sits in the middle of the square in front of the town hay scales. During the 18th and 19th centuries, the Dana Tavern stood here. The tavern was destroyed by fire in 1816. A Baptist church was built near the site of the present Presbyterian church. This Victorian Gothic building was constructed in 1876 by James Rooney as a dry and fancy goods store. (BPL.)

Fifteen years later, this image shows Harvard Square and Street, *c.* 1910. Harvard Hall has been replaced with the 1904 brick building, designed by William C. Collett. By this time, the Lowe Building had been remodeled for the Brookline National Bank. In 1902, the bank hired Peabody & Stearns to enlarge the structure. The third floor was raised and the brick storefront was replaced with stone piers. St. Mary's Church, the second edifice for the parish established in 1852, was constructed on Linden Place between 1880 and 1886. (BPC.)

The Charles Holtzer factory on Station Street, part of the Holtzer-Cabot Company, was one of Brookline's few industries. Charles Holtzer came from Germany in 1866. He operated the first telephone exchange outside Boston and built this complex starting in 1887. In 1915, the Holtzer-Cabot Company moved to Amory Street in Roxbury. The Boston and Albany Railroad built this station in 1878, after succeeding the Boston & Worcester, the original railroad starting in 1847. In 1958, the MBTA took over the line for its Highland Branch. (BPL.)

Holtzer-Cabot Company manufactured bells, alarms, annunciators, telephone equipment, and small motors. They also built, in 1891, the first electric automobile made in America for Brookline resident Fiske Warren. The second electric car Holtzer made in 1893 had a body built by Michael Quinlan, a carriage manufacturer in the village. Among the passengers are Charles Holtzer, his niece and her husband, Arthur O'Shea, the latter a long-serving executive secretary for the town. (Courtesy Museum of Transportation.)

An early 1880s view of the western end of Washington Street shows the early entrance to White Place under the bridge. In 1722, the White family bought acreage for pastures. Samuel A. Walker, a real estate auctioneer bought the land in 1846 and when he laid it out in 1848, he moved some older homes onto the first few lots. Some of the houses were built of wood from the Punch Bowl Tavern. (BPL.)

Before 1857, most of the business was below the bridge. On the right was the Good Intent Fire Station, designed by Louis Weissbein in 1870. White's Block, adjacent to the station, was typical of the wooden Mansard commercial structures in this area. The panel brick building in the center was built in the 1870s and became the representative of Brookline Village. To its left is Lyceum Hall, a wooden Greek Revival structure built by Samuel Walker in the 1840s. In 1874, Henry Ward Beecher and Frederick Douglass both lectured there. (BPL.)

This Village Square image shows the fire station, the Brookline Union building, and Walnut Street shops. The fire station, built in 1908, was designed by Freeman, Funk & Wilcox. The island shows the 1909 trolley transfer stations of the Boston Elevated Railway, whose tracks went down Boylston to the Robinson Field car barn. In the 1930s, the route was replaced by the bus line. In 1942, a WPA project removed the rails for scrap steel for the war effort. (Courtesy Joel Shield.)

Built in 1940 on the site of the 1840s Lyceum, a White Tower restaurant stood at the corner of Washington and Pearl Streets. Behind it was the town's second cinema, opened in 1937. Both buildings were demolished in 1968 for the redevelopment of this area. (BPC.)

In 1821, the Classical School was built by Richard Sullivan on Boylston Street in the Greek Revival style to prepare boys for college. After 1832, it was leased; one tenant was William Ware, author of *Zenobia* (1838). Dr. Samuel A. Shurtleff owned the property from 1838 until his death in 1873. He moved the gym to the rear and used the Classical School as his parlor. After 1881, the Shurtleff family sold the property, which was subdivided into a carriage manufacturing shop and residences. The original school was torn down in 1936. (BPL.)

The corner at Cypress and Boylston was a densely built area of multi-family houses by the late 19th century. Originally Moses Jones's estate along the village brook, it had been subdivided into an area of multi-family worker housing and stables. These triple-deckers were built in the 1890s by John Gaffey, John Lalley, and developer John J. McCormack. They were demolished in the early 1930s to make way for a service station. (BPL.)

This view of Boylston Street near the old Lincoln School in 1876 is looking east. It shows the intense development of this area that included residences, blacksmith shops, and livery establishments. This photograph was taken before the grade change in the late 1870s. Over the years, the street has been widened and lowered, and in 1933, it became a state highway. (BPL.)

Among the major businesses in Brookline Village were livery and boarding stables. By 1868, Eben Morse ran this wooden stable. Later owners were Grafton Stone, Stone and Goodspeed, and finally, Munroe Goodspeed. It stood at the bottom of Holden Street at the corner of Washington, right across from the 1873 town hall site. (BPL.)

After 1893, the livery stable added a brick veneer. Munroe Goodspeed, born in Vermont, bought out Stone's stable after being a partner for several years. He was respected for his knowledge of horses and his stable was "well-kept" with many clients, including the delivery wagons and horses of the S.S. Pierce Company. Goodspeed died in 1921. The building now houses offices and a restaurant. (BPL.)

Three

LONGWOOD AND COTTAGE FARM

Longwood and Cottage Farm are the names given to an area of Brookline laid out and developed in the early 19th century by two Boston businessmen, David Sears and Amos A. Lawrence. They understood the potential of this area as a residential neighborhood that provided a country setting close to Boston. Today, both Longwood and Cottage Farm are listed on the National Register of Historic Places.

Sears began to purchase low-lying pasture fields in the eastern section of Brookline, following the construction of the Mill Dam Road to Boston in 1821. Initially he made few improvements, but by the late 1830s, he had laid out several squares in anticipation of residential development. Longwood Mall, Mason, Knyvet, and Winthrop squares were all established by Sears. It is said he planted 14,000 trees. Longwood Mall still contains his most splendid achievement, the great beech trees imported from Europe. The name Longwood is in honor of Napoleon's estate on St. Helena. The original Sears development extended across the Muddy River into Boston, but that area has been completely altered by the construction of multi-family housing and medical facilities.

In 1850 Sears sold 200 acres of his Longwood property to William and Amos A. Lawrence. Amos Lawrence was instrumental in the construction of Beacon Street, which provided direct access from his property to Boston via the Mill Dam road. The Lawrences knew that construction of Beacon Street in Brookline was essential to open the area for businessmen who commuted daily into the city by horse and carriage. This was different from David Sears, whose family occupied the estate only during the late spring and fall between winters in Boston and summers at Nahant or Newport.

Amos A. Lawrence took the lead in developing this property, which he called "Cottage Farm." This name came to be applied to the area north of Beacon Street where both Amos and William Lawrence had their homes. Sears's name for the area, Longwood, has traditionally been retained for the section south of Beacon Street. The names for each neighborhood received formal ratification when the two railroad stations were established. The Cottage Farm station was located at the north end of Essex Street, and the Longwood station stood near the present trolley stop on Chapel Street.

Amos Lawrence restricted development in Cottage Farm, which is why much of the housing dates from the early 20th century after his death. Establishment of Amory Playground in 1903–04, and Halls Pond in 1975, has helped to preserve the sense of open space that was characteristic of the Cottage Farm of Amos Lawrence.

In contrast, the Longwood neighborhood south of Beacon Street experienced rapid development throughout the late 19th century. Longwood and Sewall Avenues, and Kent Street in particular, were lined with large and fashionable homes. A few of these have survived, especially close to the Longwood Mall. Most, however, lasted less than 40 years and were replaced by apartment blocks and smaller scale single-family homes. One of the most fashionable of the apartment complexes is the group known as Longwood Towers, constructed in 1924–25, and modeled after similar developments in Detroit and Philadelphia.

David Sears II, one of the wealthiest landowners in Boston, was primarily responsible for planning this area of Brookline as a residential neighborhood. Although he built a house for himself in 1842–43, he apparently never spent any time here, preferring his winter home on Beacon Hill or his summer cottage in Newport. He built houses for six of his children here: Frederick, Anna Amory, Ellen D'Hautville, Harriet Crowninshield, Miriam Rives, and David Jr. (BPL.)

This detail of an 1855 town map shows the entire area to the north and south of Beacon Street called Longwood, although Amos Lawrence had already begun his Cottage Farm development. There are only a few scattered houses and marshland to the east of St. Mary's Street. At that time, the town line still extended to the Charles River. (BPC.)

Of all of David Sears's children, his daughter, Anna Amory, was probably the most fond of the Brookline estate. The picturesque Gothic Revival house built in 1846 was similar to the one Edward Shaw designed for her father. A year later she wrote her father requesting additional land, stating, "I cannot carry out my wishes for its embellishment as a Country Seat nearly so satisfactorily without it, though with it, it is all I could desire. As you know, this place is now my Hobby . . . " (Courtesy Massachusetts Historical Society.)

David Sears built this Italianate villa in 1852 for his youngest daughter, Grace, who had married William Cabel Rives Jr., in 1849. The house, which cost $14,000 to build, was located on Still Street opposite Winthrop Square. In the late 19th century John Reece, an inventor of the buttonhole machine, which he patented, acquired the house. He died at age 42 in an accident in which he was attempting to save the life of an elevator operator in his newly completed factory in Boston. (Courtesy of Jenna and Aly Kidrin.)

David Sears III was one of the last of the children to build a house at Longwood. His property, located opposite Longwood Mall, at the corner of Kent and Chatham Streets, is shown in this 1933 photograph. The property is now the site of the Chatham Circle development. (BPC.)

The David Sears III house was built in 1860, and designed by Arthur Gilman. Gilman, one of the leading architects in Boston, was working on the Sears Chapel in Longwood and the Arlington Street Church in Boston at the same time. David Sears III died in 1873, only two years after his father. (BPC.)

Christ's Church in Longwood was built by David Sears II in 1860–61 as an ecumenical house of worship. Architect Arthur Gilman is said to have modeled the design on the Sears ancestral church, St. Peters in Colchester, England. Construction of this non-sectarian church was one of Sears's last contributions to the improvement of his Longwood development. This photograph, c. 1896, shows the Muddy River following the plans by the Olmsted firm. In the center of the photograph is the Longwood train station, built for the Boston & Albany Railroad, in 1894. (BPL.)

The old Longwood Avenue Bridge, c. 1896, was built before the construction of the stone bridge in 1898. This photograph shows the improvements to the Muddy River have been completed, but the wooden bridge did not conform to the picturesque design concepts the Olmsted firm developed for the Riverway Park. The local newspaper commented at the time that, "The present bridge is unsightly, is entirely out of harmony with the surroundings, and is dilapidated and unsafe." (BPL.)

Amos A. Lawrence was, like his father and namesake, successful at managing the family textile businesses. His avowed purpose in constructing his Cottage Farm development was to achieve a balance in his life and not become totally consumed with business, as his father had been. Cottage Farm provided a country retreat for a deeply religious man who was also very concerned about the "moral society" where his family resided. (BPL.)

Amos A. Lawrence hired his friend, George M. Dexter, to design a Gothic Revival stone house. Built in 1850–51, it was clearly inspired by the architecture of English country houses. This early daguerreotype was taken prior to the addition of the chapel wing, built in memory of Abraham Lincoln in 1865. The carriage barn has since been demolished. The house originally faced Essex Street at the corner of Ivy. In 1899, it was moved back on the lot and turned to face Ivy Street. (SPNEA.)

Architect George M. Dexter built a house for his daughter and son-in-law, Emily and Thomas Hall, in 1851. The Halls had one child, Maria. Known as "Minna," she grew up in the Cottage Farm neighborhood with her friend Harriet Lawrence. Minna Hall and Harriet Lawrence learned to love nature in Cottage Farm and together they founded the Massachusetts Audubon Society in 1896. Minna Hall served as a director of that organization until her death in 1951, at age 91. (BPL.)

Lawrence School on Francis Street was named after Amos A. Lawrence. Designed by Peabody & Stearns in 1874, the original section is the center of the building as it appears here c. 1896. A rapidly growing population led to additions on the west side in 1884, and the east side in 1891. This school was replaced by the present structure in 1929. (BPL.)

With the growth of Longwood as a residential neighborhood in the 1880s, several residents conceived the idea to build a clubhouse for men. Livingstone Cushing offered to build a house and rent it to club members. Architects Andrews, Jaques & Rantoul were hired to design the Riverdale Casino on Francis Street near the Lawrence School. Constructed in 1894, the Shingle Style structure was designed to look like a house, which made it compatible with the neighborhood. (Courtesy Dan Miranda.)

During the 19th century the name "casino" meant a clubhouse and did not necessarily have gambling connotations. These sketches of the interior, probably supplied by the architects, show various details, including a "Ladies Reception Room." The casino, like most clubs in the 19th century, was segregated by sex. The club included a billiard room with four tables in the ell, bowling alleys in the basement, and a meeting room on the second floor. (BPC.)

Benjamin F. Keith was one of the most prominent residents of Brookline at the turn of the century. He is credited with originating the idea of a theater with a continuous vaudeville performance rather than short acts serving as an adjunct to some other attraction. The first full-length vaudeville show was held in Boston in 1885. By the time of his death in 1914, B.F. Keith owned, solely or in partnership, 20 vaudeville theaters around the country. Numerous other theaters handled their bookings through the Keith booking office in New York. (BPL.)

Benjamin Keith grew up in New Hampshire and worked on a farm in western Massachusetts before becoming involved in show business at age 18. With his success in establishing vaudeville theaters in Boston, Keith purchased an older house on the corner of Kent Street and Sewall Avenue. He had it extensively remodeled into a palatial Colonial Revival residence in 1894 by architect William Ralph Emerson. The house was demolished in 1938. (BPL.)

One of the most unusual buildings in Brookline is the Dutch House on Netherlands Road. Originally built for the World's Colombian Exposition in Chicago in 1893, it was the pavilion for the Van Houten Cocoa Company and a copy of the 1591 Franeker Town Hall in Holland. When the exposition ended, Charles B. Appleton purchased the building at auction and had it reassembled on this site in Brookline in 1894 with a new concrete exterior finish to imitate brick and stone. At the time, the Olmsted-designed improvements to the Muddy River had just been completed and the building had a clear view of the new park. (BPL.)

The house of George H. Wrightman, completed in 1902, was clearly intended to take advantage of the type of site afforded by David Sears's original layout of Longwood. The Wrightman Mansion is directly opposite the Longwood Mall with its magnificent beech trees. By taking advantage of the rectangular park, the architects, Shepley, Rutan & Coolidge, were able to provide the house with a grand approach on an axis with Chatham Street. The grounds of the property itself were laid out by the Olmsted Brothers. (Courtesy Shepley, Bulfinch, Richardson, and Abbott.)

Four

SOUTH BROOKLINE

As early as the 1790s the hilly farmland of south Brookline attracted wealthy Bostonians in search of country retreats between winters in Boston and summers at Nahant. One of the wealthiest men to build a house in Brookline was Thomas Handasyd Perkins, the "merchant prince" of Boston. He acquired a farm in 1799, and built a house in 1805–06. Other prominent merchants who maintained country homes in south Brookline included Jonathan Jackson, Stephen Higginson, Samuel G. Perkins, and Jonathan Mason. Retired sea captains Adam Babcock, Nathaniel Ingersoll, and Isaac Cook also acquired property here. These men constructed wooden dwellings, usually in a picturesque style that was compatible with the relaxed, informal ambiance of Brookline.

By the 1840s, these "country gentlemen" were becoming famous for their displays of horticulture on their country estates. Moreover, the houses they built began to reflect the sophisticated historical styles designed by leading Boston architects. Italianate and Gothic villas became especially popular. Children of these Bostonians typically built homes near the original family estates. T.H. Perkins provided land for his daughter and son-in-law, Samuel Cabot, in 1838. Ignatius Sargent, who erected a stone house around 1844, sold land to his daughter and son-in-law, James Codman, and his son, Charles Sprague Sargent, who built houses nearby.

Toward the close of the 19th century, the country estates of these part-time residents tended to become larger with formal gardens and grounds designed by landscape architects. Italian Renaissance gardens were especially popular components that were planned to be fully integrated with the house and grounds. The estates of the Spragues and the Andersons were two of the most famous examples.

Attempts to construct multi-family housing in south Brookline were generally resisted by the owners of the large estates. In 1893, John J. McCormick proposed to offer 100 house lots for sale on Clyde Street near the country club. This sub-division was strongly resisted and only a small cluster of houses was actually built. Ironically, Francis Ouimet, one of Brookline's most famous golfers, grew up in this development. More typical were neighborhoods of upper-middle-class homes, such as those built near Lee and Dudley Streets, or around Sargent's Pond during the 1920s as it became more common to commute to Boston daily by automobile. Large sections of open space in south Brookline were preserved from residential development by the country club, founded in 1882, and the Putterham Meadows golf course, created by the town in 1930.

The sub-division of large estates for single-family homes began in the early 1900s and continues today. A few estates were acquired by private schools and religious institutions, which sometimes preserved the original mansion and portions of the open space. For example, the estate built by Anna Sears is now the Dexter School, while the house and grounds of Southwood, the former Barthold Schlesinger residence, has been preserved by the Holy Transfiguration Monastery. The Louis Cabot mansion also survived while owned by a religious order, but was demolished in 1996 after it fell into private hands.

Believed to have been constructed in 1772, the Widow Harris House is one of the few surviving 18th-century buildings in Brookline. Hannah Winchester Harris died in this house in 1805, after which her daughter and son-in-law, Hannah and Elijah Child, resided here. Their son, Timothy Child, owned the house until the mid-19th century. It eventually became part of the Larz Anderson estate and is now part of Larz Anderson Park. (BPL.)

Green Hill is the best-known example of early 19th-century country homes said to have been inspired by the plantations of the West Indies. Constructed in 1806 for Nathaniel Ingersoll, Green Hill was eventually purchased by John L. Gardner in 1842. Although Gardner made horticultural improvements as early as 1844, it was his daughter-in-law, Isabella Stewart Gardner, who made Green Hill particularly famous for its Italian and Japanese gardens. Mrs. Gardner's improvements to the estate occurred primarily in the 1890s. (SPNEA.)

Captain Isaac Cook built this cottage for his son, Thomas Drew Cook, in 1827. This extraordinary cottage is a very unusual early example of a house designed in a Gothic style. When their son died at age 20, before he could live here, Captain Cook and his wife moved into the house and created a romantic Victorian landscape. The little Gothic cottage was nestled into the base of a hill and included a stream and waterfall just beyond the raised verandah. The Cooks lived here for the remainder of their lives. (BPL.)

During the late 1840s, a major change occurred in the design of country homes built by wealthy Bostonians. The informality of Green Hill gave way to historic European styles, such as the 1846 villa built for John Eliot Thayer. Thayer had Richard Upjohn design this Italianate country house in Brookline and a Beacon Hill town house in the same style. Thayer was a founder of Kidder, Peabody and was appointed to the United States Senate to succeed Daniel Webster in 1850. The Dudley Street house burned in 1948. (SPNEA.)

Charles Sprague Sargent, founder of the Arnold Arboretum, created what was one of the most admired country estates outside Boston in the late 19th century. Thomas Lee had started his estate, called "Holm Lea," in the early 19th century. Sargent enlarged the gardens begun by Lee. Particularly well known were the rhododendrons, first planted in large numbers in 1866. The house no longer stands but Sargent's Pond survives and is preserved in a land trust. (BPL.)

A charity bazaar was held at Holm Lea on June 6, 1908. Money was raised to benefit the Welcome House and Industrial Home for Women. This institution, backed by many of the leading Boston families, offered shelter for homeless women and training to make them independent. Charles S. Sargent is the man with the beard. (BPL.)

The charity bazaar at Holm Lea included food and clothing booths, games, and sideshows like Punch and Judy. The swan boats from the Boston Public Garden were also imported to Sargent's Pond for the day. (BPL.)

Built for George Bacon in 1861, this house was named "Sevenels" by Augustus Lowell, who acquired the property in 1866, along with his wife and five children—the seven "L's." Augustus married Katherine Lawrence, daughter of Abbott. The five Lowell children were Percival, the astronomer who discovered Pluto; Abbott, who became president of Harvard University; Katherine, who married a cousin of Theodore Roosevelt; Elizabeth; and Amy, the poet. The garden was an endless source of inspiration for Amy's poems. (SPNEA.)

Amy Lowell was born at Sevenels in 1874. She spent much of her childhood in the third floor nursery of Sevenels. This room, which she called her "sky parlor," was where she later wrote much of her poetry. She was widely recognized in the early part of the 20th century for her poetry, which included experiments in free verse. She never married, and her first poem was published in 1910, ten years after her father's death. In 1912, she published a volume of verse, *A Dome of Many Colored Glass*. (BPL.)

Nathaniel Murdock, a local housewright, constructed this house for Deacon Joshua Clark in 1810. Frederick Law Olmsted purchased it in 1881. He had come to Boston to advise on the development of the park system for the Back Bay Fens in 1878. Until his retirement in 1895, Olmsted worked out of the office wing he added on to the old Deacon Clark house. The Clark house was altered and enlarged in a way that preserved the old lines of the house, yet reflected Olmsted's concern that buildings should be in harmony with the landscape. Successive Olmsted firms continued to work at this location until 1979. (Courtesy National Park Service, Frederick Law Olmsted National Historic Site.)

Although not as well known as his stepfather, John C. Olmsted played an important role in the work of the firm. After graduating from Yale, John joined the firm and became a full partner in 1888. With his half-brother Frederick, John produced many important landscape designs in the tradition of their father. Many landscape historians recognize that John Charles Olmsted made a major contribution to the success of the firm. (Courtesy National Park Service, Frederick Law Olmsted National Historic Site.)

John C. Olmsted purchased "Cliffside" for his home in order to be near the Olmsted office. The house was built for Samuel G. Perkins, brother of Thomas Handasyd Perkins, one of the wealthiest merchants in Boston. However, it is not clear who built sections of this house, Samuel Perkins or two subsequent owners, Waldo Maynard and William Dwight Jr. Much of the present structure, with its combination of double-pitched gable ends and mansard tower, appears to date from the 1850s. (Courtesy Jenna and Aly Kidrin.)

Known simply as "The Country Club," Brookline's long-standing private institution dates to its formation in April 1882 (conceived in 1860). As reported in the Brookline newspaper at the time, "The general idea is to have a comfortable club-house for the use of members with their families, a simple restaurant, bedrooms, bowling alley, lawn tennis, a racing track, etc." The clubhouse was originally the country home of Dr. William Spooner, built about 1802 with subsequent alterations. The *c.* 1910 postcard view shown here reflects remodeling by Ball & Dabney, Chapman & Frazer, and Andrews, Jaques & Rantoul. (Courtesy Tim Sullivan.)

An important early component of the Country Club was the riding track, as club members were interested in trotting races, fox hunting, steeplechase courses, and polo. The first grandstand was built in 1882, but this was replaced by the impressive Neo-classical grandstand and viewing stand shown here. James T. Kelley designed these structures in 1904, which cost $25,000. They were replaced in 1926, before the riding track was eliminated altogether. (SPNEA.)

Francis Desales Ouimet was born in Brookline in 1893 and grew up in the small working class neighborhood across from the Country Club. He learned to play golf from watching others and practicing on his own in the early morning hours. At the age of 20 he entered the U.S. Open that was held at the Country Club in 1913 and won, defeating two veteran British golfers. Shown here, from left to right are his caddie, Eddie Lowery, and Francis Ouimet. In 1914, he won the U.S. Amateur and the French Open. (Courtesy Ouimet Museum.)

William F. Weld built the first large summer home on the hill that is now Larz Anderson Park. Weld's niece, Isabel Anderson, acquired the Weld property in 1899, at which time she and her husband began extensive improvements. The house that was built in 1886–87 was extensively enlarged by Little & Browne, architects. Isabel's husband, Larz Anderson, was in the foreign service, serving as minister to Belgium and ambassador to Japan in the Taft administration. The estate in Brookline served as their country retreat. (BPC.)

Called "the Garden of Weld," Charles Platt designed the Italian garden that was located on top of the hill opposite the east facade of the mansion in 1901. Isabel Anderson was chiefly responsible for the improvements to the house and grounds in Brookline. Born Isabel Weld Perkins in 1876, she married Larz Anderson in 1897. Her gardens were frequently opened to the poor and for charity benefits. Upon her death in 1948, her Brookline property was bequeathed to the town to be used for educational and recreational purposes. (Courtesy Museum of Transportation.)

Larz Anderson's major passion was vehicles—carriages and automobiles. The large stables, which are now the Museum of Transportation, were built in 1889 for William Weld and designed by Franz Zerrahn. This photo shows a 1905 Walter Tractor, which was designed to pull a brougham that was formerly drawn by horses. (Courtesy Museum of Transportation.)

Pictured is Mrs. Anderson riding in her Memorial Day "float" with an unidentified Uncle Sam. She won first prize. (Courtesy Museum of Transportation.)

Charles F. Sprague had just been elected to Congress when he hired architects Little, Browne & Moore to build "Faulkner Farm" off Newton Street. The house was later enlarged with a third story and masonry veneer. Sprague and his wife, the former Anna Pratt, hired Charles Platt to design a magnificent Italianate garden for their estate. This was Platt's first major landscape design in which the garden and grounds were fully integrated with the house. (BPL.)

One feature of the large country estate in Brookline for which very little evidence survives are greenhouses to cultivate all the plants. The greenhouses of Faulkner Farm were typical of these sprawling horticultural complexes. (BPL.)

The Putterham School now stands in Larz Anderson Park, where it was moved in 1955. As shown on its original site in this photograph, it was located on Newton Street near the Country Club. The frame of this building is believed to date from 1768, although it was enlarged and remodeled in 1840, 1847, and 1855. Visible behind the school was the almshouse, constructed in 1883. (SPNEA.)

Newton and Grove Street was the location for several town facilities. In addition to the Putterham School, which closed in 1922, and the almshouse, or poorhouse, closed in 1931, was a high service water pumping station, built in 1885. It was also the location of the Contagious Disease Hospital, which closed in 1954. The *Brookline Town Atlas* of 1927 shows these structures and their location near the Country Club. (BPC.)

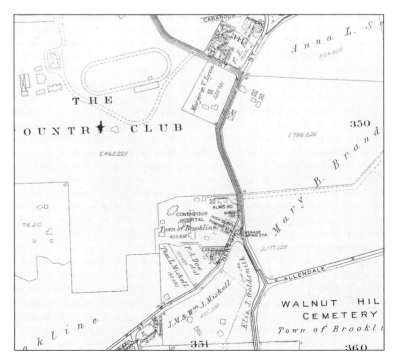

The Contagious Disease Hospital was established in 1901. In 1915, a separate structure for tuberculosis patients was constructed. Designed by Harold Field Kellogg, the building featured flanking wards that enabled patients to benefit from country air. (BPL.)

In 1943, the Town of Brookline appointed a long range planning committee to deal with the problems of returning service members after the war. An outcome of this effort was the Hancock Village residential development. This so-called "garden village" concept was derived from similar housing projects in Washington, D.C. The development, which was constructed from 1946–49 by the John Hancock Life Insurance Company, was designed by Washington architect Louis Justement. (Courtesy Joel Shield.)

Five

PILL HILL AND
THE POINT

Pill Hill, or High Street Hill as it was more formally called, assumed its present configuration in 1844, when Brookline annexed Boston-owned land extending eastwards from High Street to Pond. As early as the 17th century, however, Walnut Street, one of the neighborhood's major routes, played an important role in the history and development of Brookline. Once a part of the old Sherburne Road, Walnut Street was a link in the only westward route from Boston.

One of the developers of this area, Samuel Philbrick, owned the granite house at 182 Walnut Street. With his son Edward he developed Upland Road, Maple Street, and the center section of Walnut Street. Edward Philbrick graduated Harvard College in 1846, became a civil engineer, working on the Hoosac Tunnel in 1870, the Brookline Waterworks in 1874, the landfill plan for South End, and the design of the foundations of both the Boston Public Library and Trinity Church. Some of this land Philbrick sold in the 1860s, and in the 1870s, he built several houses on the Walnut Street and Upland Road.

Another part of Pill Hill was developed by the Brookline Land Company, formed in 1860. It was the neighborhood's largest individual landowner in the second half of the 19th century, buying 80 acres stretching from Brookline Village to Jamaica Pond and from the Muddy River to High Street. By 1876, 30 acres had been sold and 2 miles of streets and avenues built.

The Land Company wished to preserve the "high class" quality of the neighborhood through deed restrictions that prevented "any occupation or erection of any building, which could work injury or annoyance to residents." It coordinated its plans with Frederick Law Olmsted's for the Muddy River Improvement (part of the Emerald Necklace) to enhance its private efforts. This resulted in the sale of company land for the creation of Leverett Pond and Olmsted Park.

Many of these property owners hired well-established and respected architects to create a visually harmonious neighborhood which now includes fine examples of structures designed in the latest architectural styles. Occupying many of the homes during the 19th and 20th centuries have been leaders in the fields of politics, education, science, and the arts. In fact, the name Pill Hill derives from the number of doctors who lived here in the early 20th century. Pill Hill is both a National Register District and a Local Historic District.

"The Point," the area below Pill Hill on the south side, was developed in the late 19th century for multi-family housing. This began in 1871, when a group of small working-class houses were moved from Bradley's Hill (now Brigington Road) to Hart Street. Several other small, single-family homes were built on the east side of Chestnut Street, and in 1873, the town stables were constructed on the corner of Cypress and Kendall Streets. The West End Railroad Company erected a car barn in 1894. These developments set the pattern for this area of Brookline as a working-class neighborhood predominantly occupied by Irish Americans.

"The Farm" is the name given to the area below the north slope of Pill Hill. Named for the Ward Farm, this neighborhood was formed by High Street on the west, Boylston Street on the north, Pond Avenue on the east, and Pill Hill on the south. The multi-family housing constructed in this area was completely razed for urban redevelopment in the 1960s and is now the site of the Brook House and cooperative apartment blocks.

John Tappan, along with his brother Lewis, later became a famous New York merchant and abolitionist, and constructed this house on Walnut Street in 1821–22. In 1829, Samuel Philbrick, another leading abolitionist, acquired the house. Philbrick invited famous abolitionists, such as the Grimke sisters and Theodore Dwight, to stay here. Two fugitive slaves, William and Ellen Crafts, were harbored in the house in 1848 on their way to Canada. After Samuel Philbrick's death in 1859, his son Edward was instrumental in the development of Pill Hill as a residential neighborhood. (BPL.)

Located on the hill above Walnut Street, this house was built by Alfred Winsor in 1857. In the summer of 1919, Mrs. Alfred Winsor, who had been a director of the Brookline Day Nursery, provided her house as a convalescent home for servicemen. In doing so, she afforded many young men from around the country a chance to recuperate in an idyllic Brookline setting. (BPL.)

Walnut Place, a private way on Pill Hill, is one of the most secluded residential areas in Brookline. This photograph, *c.* 1875, shows the home of the Stevenson sisters, who are standing in the yard. Presumably, it is their mother in the second floor window. (BPL.)

Several Brookline residents met in 1860 to incorporate a church dedicated to the teachings of Emanuel Swedenborg, known as the doctrines of the "New Jerusalem." They agreed to build a church on a triangular piece of land off High Street. Many of the "Swedenborgians" in Brookline were involved in the Brookline Land Company, which was attempting to develop the eastern slope of Pill Hill. William Robert Ware, who was in a brief partnership with Edward Philbrick, designed the stone church, which was built in 1861–62. This view of the church dates from about 1875. (BPL.)

The house, built by Edward Stanwood on High Street, is one of the outstanding examples of the Queen Anne style in Brookline. It was erected in 1879–80 and designed by Clarence Luce. Edward Stanwood was for many years the editor of the *Boston Daily Advertiser*, and a children's magazine, *The Youths Companion*. This design for Stanwood's house was published in the *American Architect and Building News*, only one of several Pill Hill houses to appear in an architectural journal. (BPL.)

Pill Hill got its name for the number of physicians who lived there, one of whom was George K. Sabine. Dr. Sabine built this house in 1882, at 30 Irving and the corner of Upland. The Queen Anne house is attributed to Cabot & Chandler. Dr. Sabine, who died in 1927, served on a number of boards and committees relating to the health and welfare of town citizens. He was especially well known for his work on behalf of returning veterans after WW I. The Sabine house was demolished in 1941. (Courtesy Caroline Oveson Lovelace.)

Edgehill Road is a *cul-de-sac* on Pill Hill with houses that originally had dramatic views toward Boston over-looking Leverett Pond. This house, photographed about 1885, was constructed for Samuel Cabot in 1881. Cabot was a nephew of Edward Cabot, whose firm, Cabot & Chandler, designed this unusual Shingle Style house. There are several architecturally distinctive houses on this street, including the home built by Robert Swain Peabody of Peabody & Stearns. (BPL.)

The Brookline Friendly Society has its origins in the Free Temperance Reading Room organized by the Brookline Christian Women's Temperance Society in 1878. Led by Anna Stearns, this women's group spawned the Brookline Union in 1886. The Brookline Union sought to combat poverty, intemperance, crime, and violence by banning the sale of liquor, while recognizing the need to provide educational and cultural activities for the town's citizens. Located at the corner of Walnut and High Streets, the Brookline Union Building was constructed in 1887–89 and designed by Thomas Minot Clark. (BPL.)

The original building for the Free Hospital for Women was constructed in 1894–95 just below Edgehill Road. The architects were Shaw & Hunnewell. The hospital was historically important for its innovative approaches to medicine, especially for its emphasis on gynecology. The site over-looking Leverett Pond and the Olmsted-designed park was important as the beneficial effects of light and fresh air for hospital patients was well recognized at the time. (Courtesy Tim Sullivan.)

Edward C. Cabot, architect of the Boston Athenaeum, founding member and president of the Boston Society of Architects, and designer of a number of houses on Pill Hill and elsewhere in Brookline, lived on an estate between Chestnut Street and Jamaica Road. His family were longtime residents of Brookline and the home of his parents, which he designed, survives on Warren Street. Unfortunately, no images have been discovered of either of the two houses he built in the Point, which were demolished in 1947 for a public housing project. (BPL.)

John Ward's farm was located on Walter Avenue, near Pond Avenue, now the site of the Brook House. The house shown in this photograph was probably constructed in 1849, although portions of the older house may have been incorporated into a larger dwelling. Beginning in 1918, the house was used by the Brookline Friendly Society as a Community Health Center. It was demolished about 1959 as part of the urban renewal of "The Farm" neighborhood. (BPL.)

During the late 19th century the neighborhood called "The Farm" included several streets with multi-family housing. A small two-room school was constructed in 1883 and enlarged in 1886. Parsons School was one of two that featured experimental "Fresh Air Rooms" in 1911. The windows and doors for the second grade class were kept open. Children were given khaki sleeping bags and slippers to wear. The temperature was not allowed to fall below 55 degrees. The Parsons School was demolished in 1944. (BPC.)

Pictured above is the corner of Pond Avenue and Morss Avenue in "the Farm" neighborhood. At this corner, Michael Rourke acquired a building lot and began to construct three family tenements. The first was built in 1893, followed by the one on the corner three years later. Both structures were designed by Samuel Rantin, an architect who specialized in wood frame, multi-family housing. (BPC.)

A school garden program was established in Brookline in 1903. Children between the ages of 12 and 15 were each responsible for a 9-by-7-foot garden. Gardens were established for Lincoln, Parson, Winthrop, and Sewall schools. In the background is Sewall School. These garden programs were organized for schools with children who would not have an opportunity to learn about gardening outside of a classroom. (BPL.)

The Boston Elevated Railway Company ran a streetcar line up Boylston Street to Cypress. The line followed Cypress up to a car barn at the corner of Franklin Street in 1894. The original wood and brick structure included an ornamental clock tower on one corner. This building was demolished in 1934 and is now the site of Robinson Park. (Courtesy Hall Silloway.)

In 1891, Amory and William Lawrence, as executors of the will of Sarah Lawrence, established a trust "for the purpose of providing improved dwellings for the poorer classes at reasonable rentals." The trust formalized the efforts of Sarah Lawrence to build housing for the poor in Brookline. Two buildings, erected in 1892 on High Street Place, were called the "Groton" and the "Kansan" after places important in the history of the Lawrence family. Two other buildings had already been erected on Roberts Street and two on Pearl Street in 1891. (BPC.)

The neighborhood called "the Point" originated in 1871, when a group of working class cottages were moved to Hart Street. By the 1890s, the three-family house was typical for the neighborhood. This house on Franklin Street, erected in 1899, was designed by J.H. Pineo, a contractor who built a number of multi-family homes in Brookline. (Courtesy Joel Shield.)

Six

TOWN GOVERNMENT

Town government is located in the Brookline Village/Cypress Street area. This became the locus of town government and the town's commercial center in the late 1840s. When the second town hall was built on Washington Street, the change moved the civic center away from Town Green. While the commercial center shifted to Coolidge Corner at the turn of the century, this area continues to be the municipal center of Brookline. The municipal service buildings were constructed on the land between Holden and School Streets, containing the town halls, the public library, Pierce Grammar and Primary Schools, the original high school, the police station, and the courthouse. The area around the high school, between the MBTA tracks and Cypress Street, Tappan Street, and Greenough Street is the home to the high school, the manual-training school, the municipal gymnasium, the public baths, and one of the early municipal playgrounds.

The town government area reflects the evolution of government and its responsibilities to changing times. The early years after independence from Boston were spent building the new community. In the first year, nine town officer positions were created: constable, selectmen, town clerk, assessors, tithingman, highway surveyors, fence viewers, overseers of the common lands, and hayward, or field drivers. When Brookline was granted full independence in 1705, five selectmen were chosen to perform administrative business with help from town meeting committees. The selectmen and town meeting members oversaw the transformation of Brookline from an agricultural community to a residential suburb; from Yankee farmers to Irish and German immigrants in the 19th century to a community with over 25 nationalities, all contributing to make Brookline a dynamic community.

The 19th century brought major changes. The town fought off annexation attempts by Boston from 1870 to 1880. Population increased dramatically and there was an expansion of town government. By 1900, eight new town office positions were added—most appointed and not elected. As in much of American society, services became professionalized—the fire department, the police department, and the engineering department. The increase in population created a major issue on how to maintain the town meeting form. By 1899, the November town meeting was too large for the town hall and many voters had to be excluded. The option of changing to a city form of government was raised, but Brookline voters rejected it. Alfred D. Chandler, a Brookline citizen, developed a system of representative town meeting as early as 1897. The town adopted this change in 1915. The town meeting moved to the high school in 1944.

The 19th and 20th centuries saw the continuation of involvement of the inhabitants of Brookline, many who contributed personally and professionally to Brookline's civic and cultural life. Other inhabitants filled the ranks of the police and fire departments and served as town meeting members, commission appointees, and town staff, many volunteers contributing their expertise, time, and commitment. This tradition of an active and involved citizenry working for the good of the community continues today.

The first library building was built on the present-day site in 1866. The library, established in 1857 with one thousand volumes, was initially located in the lower hall of the 1845 town house. Brookline was one of the first communities in Massachusetts to accept legislation allowing taxes to be used for a free public library. Louis Weissbein was chosen for his design of the red brick & stone trim building. It opened in October 1869 with 12,000 volumes. In this photograph, you can also see the Matthews house and the high school. (BPL.)

Located behind the library, this Italianate structure was the first high school building in Brookline. A high school had been established in 1843 with classes in the old 1824 town house on Walnut Street and in the 1844 town house. By 1856, a committee approved this lot and hired Joseph L. Richards as architect. Dedicated on October 31, 1856, it was built in part with money donated by Edward Devotion. The first floor had separate entrances for boys and girls. It was demolished in 1902. (BPL.)

A photograph shows a view of the interior of the library in 1876. In 1905, it was decided that a new building was needed and another design competition was held. Sturgis & Barton were selected for their design of the present Classical Revival building. (BPL.)

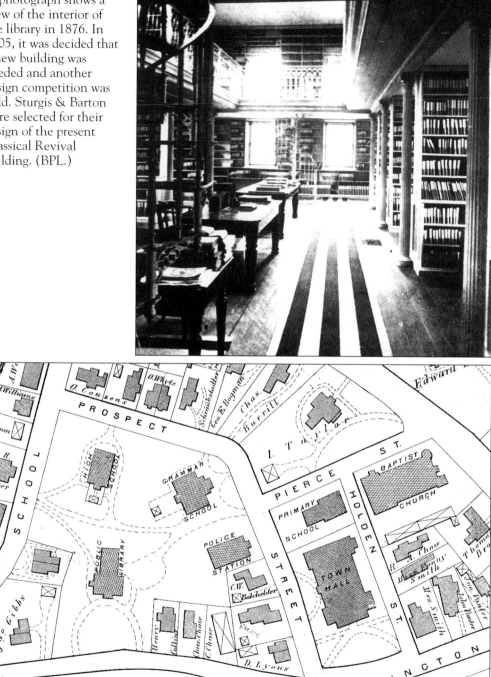

This map from the 1874 atlas of the civic center area shows the location of the public buildings. The pubic library is in the same location as the present one; the town hall is at the corner of Holden which was also the site of the courthouse and police station; the high school and Pierce Primary are behind; the police station is the moved 1844 town house. The town hall is the Victorian Gothic, which was dedicated one year before.

In April 1855, a new, four-room school was dedicated, named after the longtime First Parish minister and former school committee chair, John Pierce. Designed by John F. Edwards, it contained desks and chairs for 48 students. It quickly became overcrowded and students were sent to other locations. This is a photograph of the school and students taken in 1876. It was enlarged and altered in 1899–1900 by Julius Schweinfurth. Sections of the original school are still visible behind the existing building. (BPL.)

Pictured is the corridor in the Classical Revival Pierce School on School Street, built in 1900 from designs of Julius Schweinfurth. In the late 19th and early 20th century, many schools were filled with replicas of classical art to enhance learning and art appreciation. This photograph shows a statue of Diana, the huntress. (BPC.)

This imposing Victorian Gothic edifice was dedicated on Washington's birthday in 1873 to an audience of two thousand. Designed by Samuel J.F. Thayer, the cornerstone was laid in May 1871 with a tin memento box. It was portrayed in municipal textbooks as America's ideal town hall. It became a focal point of civic and community life, voting, town business, instruction, town meetings, caucuses, lectures, concerts, theatricals, and balls. In 1963, both this and the old police station were demolished to make way for the present town hall. (BPL.)

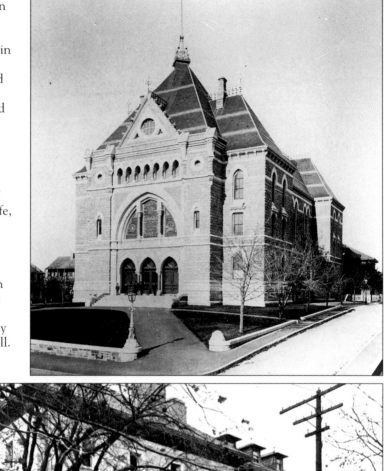

Pictured is the old police station/courthouse and the old town hall. The wooden building in the rear was the second town hall, originally built on Washington Street in 1844. This Greek Revival edifice represented the governmental and population shift to the Village area. The Classical Revival building at the corner was the new police station and courthouse designed in 1899 by Julius Schweinfurth of yellow brick and granite. The upper floor was often used for the Brookline Evening School, lectures, and the Ladies Industrial Association. The iron lanterns now hang at the new police station and the carved seal is in Harvard Square. (BPL.)

F. Joseph Untersee was the architect of the public bath and the gymnasium. He was born in Switzerland and received his training at the Polytechical School in Stuttgart, Germany. He also designed several commercial and residential buildings in Brookline. (BPL.)

This photograph of the interior of the gymnasium was taken in the 1910s. (BPL.)

Pictured above are the twin buildings of the bathhouse and gym designed by F. Joseph Untersee located on Cypress Street. The bathhouse was most likely the first municipally operated one in the country, opening January 1, 1897. Known affectionately as "the tank," it was replaced in 1958. The new gymnasium was completed in 1906, also designed by Joseph Untersee. Based on the earlier plans, it now included a lighting, heating, and power plant for the nearby municipal buildings. It burned Christmas Day 1962. (BPL.)

The bathhouse had two indoor tanks with the floor of the large pool mosaic tiling and marble steps at each end. The interior had lettering that included quotations from poems and names of famous swimmers, including Ulysses, Leander, Charlemagne, and Franklin. Renovations in 1899 added a hair drying room for women. Exhibitions of swimming exercise and polo were held. In 1949, a water pageant was held with a Cape Cod fishing theme. A group of anglers met here every Thursday for a bait casting club. (BPL.)

The second high school building stood on the site of the present one at the corner of Tappan and Greenough Streets. This Romanesque Revival building sits on land bought from the Blake estate and was designed by Andrews, Jaques & Rantoul in red eastern pressed brick and Maynard sandstone. The landscaping was done by Olmsted, Olmsted & Eliot. Soon after its opening, the tower was struck by lightning. In 1921, Kilham & Hopkins were hired to enlarge the school. When the old 1893 building burned in 1936, Kilham, Hopkins & Greeley designed a new center section the next year. (SPNEA.)

PLAYGROUND, BROOKLINE, MASS.

Cypress Field and the Brookline Avenue Playground are considered the first sites in the country acquired for municipal playground purposes. A committee of seven was appointed by the moderator in 1871 to procure one or more lots of land for public commons, suitable for playgrounds, in situations convenient to the schools of the town. The committee recommended two parcels: the Brookline Avenue Playground and a lot, bounded on Cypress Street. By 1880, the Brookline Athletic Club had built a track and seats for sports exhibitions. Over the years, Cypress Field has been the site of many activities, including ice skating, track meets, town celebrations, graduations, and baseball and football games. (Courtesy Joel Shield.)

Seven

ASPINWALL HILL AND BEACONSFIELD

Aspinwall Hill is named after one of the oldest Brookline families. Peter Aspinwall purchased land near the present St. Paul Street and Aspinwall Avenue from William Colborne in 1650. His great-grandson, Dr. William Aspinwall, acquired 87 acres on what became Aspinwall Hill in 1788, and he built a house there in 1803. Before 1880, there were few other houses in the area. The only other one on the upper part of the hill was built by Lewis Tappan in the 1820s, whose property extended down the hill to Greenough Street. On the south side of the hill, along Tappan Street, was another estate that belonged to William I. Bowditch.

There were plans to subdivide the top of the hill as early as 1857, however, actual development did not begin until 1880. At that time, Frederick Law Olmsted was hired to make preliminary plans for the arrangement of streets and house lots. Gardner Road, built in 1881, was the first street to be laid out. Landscape architect Ernest W. Bowditch, whose father William lived on Tappan Street, revised the spiral road system suggested by Olmsted in 1883. His plans resulted in the construction of Rawson Road, Winthrop Road, Addington Road, and Colbourne Crescent.

The first street to be built, Gardner Road, had the largest concentration of new houses. Several large homes in the Queen Anne style and Shingle Style were constructed during the late 1880s and early 1890s. Others followed on sites farther up the hill; designed by prominent Boston firms, such as Peabody & Stearns, Hartwell & Richardson, Chapman & Frazer, William G. Preston, E.A.P. Newcomb, and Cabot & Chandler. This created an enclave of wealthy homes for Boston businesspeople similar in character to Pill Hill. By 1893, there were 17 substantial houses built on Gardner Road alone. Unlike Pill Hill, however, most of the large 19th-century buildings are no longer standing. Speculative houses and apartment blocks began to be built on the hill as early as the 1890s, especially toward Beacon Street. Housing development projects in the 1920s and 1930s resulted in a subdivision of much of Aspinwall Hill into smaller house lots. At the same time, the Blake Estate between Gardner Road and Greenough Street was also subdivided. Unlike Pill Hill or Fisher Hill, large single-family lots did not long survive on Aspinwall Hill.

On the north slope of Aspinwall Hill, extending down to Beacon Street, was one of the most unusual neighborhood developments in Brookline. Called "Beaconsfield Terrace," this was the idea of Eugene Knapp, a wool importer who invested his fortune in this endeavor. In addition to town houses, he built stables, a casino, a playground, tennis courts, and a 6-acre park for the enjoyment of all the residents. With the demand for housing in this area, the parks and clubhouse quickly gave way to new town houses and an apartment hotel.

Dr. William Aspinwall lived in the 17th-century family home on Aspinwall Avenue before constructing this house in 1803. He had acquired 40 acres on what became Aspinwall Hill in 1788, but did not build a new house for himself until he was 60 years old. The Aspinwall house, demolished in 1900, stood on the hill over-looking Washington Street, about where the present Gardner Road is intersected by Winthrop. In 1896, William Aspinwall's great-grandson, Thomas Aspinwall, built a house on Hawthorn Road on Pill Hill, which closely resembled the family home on Aspinwall Hill. (BPL.)

Susanna Aspinwall, the youngest daughter of William Aspinwall, was married to Lewis Tappan, of the *Amistad* incident, in the doctor's house on Aspinwall Hill in 1813. This miniature portrait of Susanna Tappan was made at the time of her wedding. (*Brookline Historical Society Proceedings.*)

George Baty Blake came from Vermont at age 13 as an orphan. He worked as a clerk in a dry goods store. As a young man he joined an importing business, and eventually became an international banker. In that capacity he negotiated loans for the government with the Rothchilds and Barings firms during the opening months of the Civil War. He died in 1875. (BPL.)

Lewis Tappan, the famous abolitionist, built this house in the 1820s. His brother John also constructed a stone house on Walnut Street at the same time. Lewis Tappan moved to New York City a few years after building his Brookline house. In 1847, George Baty Blake acquired it, and probably added the third story, cupola, and porte-cochere. His Brookline estate occupied the southern half of Aspinwall Hill between Gardner Road and Greenough Street. (BPL.)

Ernest W. Bowditch grew up on his father's estate on Tappan Street on Aspinwall Hill. Born in 1850, he trained as a civil engineer, and worked during the formative years of the development of landscape architecture. Ernest Bowditch's practice combined civil engineering with the actual planning of developments. Not surprisingly, he was involved in the design of both major developments near his boyhood home. Bowditch played a major role in planning the Aspinwall Land Company property and the Beaconsfield Development. (Courtesy Earle G. Shettleworth Jr.)

Pictured above is Gardner Road at the intersection of Washington Street, c. 1897. These houses on Gardner Road were newly built at the time of this photograph. To the right, not visible in the photograph, is the old Aspinwall House. The house in the foreground was built for shoe manufacturer Arthur Jones in 1894–95, Eugene Clark architect. The house on the left edge of the photo fronts Washington Street. (BPL.)

Amasa Clark and John D. Sturtevant both hired architect William G. Preston to design their Gardner Road houses. Both men were in the same woolen manufacturing business, and Clark married Sturtevant's daughter. The Clark house on the right, was built in 1883–84; Sturtevant's house, at the corner of Winthrop, dates from 1885–86. The two houses illustrate the 19th-century grandeur that characterized much of Aspinwall Hill. (Courtesy Jenna and Aly Kidrin.)

At the top of Aspinwall Hill one of the largest estates was owned by Harry Hartley in 1902 on Rawson Road. Like Clark and Sturtevant, Hartley was in the wool business. His Chapman & Frazer-designed house became the home of William Cardinal O'Connell from 1916 to 1927. Subsequently, the carriage barn was turned into a chapel and the property became a friary for the Order of St. Francis. (SPNEA.)

Eugene Knapp, the developer of "Beaconsfield Terraces," lived on this 9-acre estate at the corner of Beacon and Tappan Streets. He acquired the house in 1880 and extensively enlarged it five years later. With the widening of Beacon Street in the late 1880s, Knapp invested his entire fortune in his Beaconsfield development. The house is now the site of a grocery store. (BPL.)

This view of the Beaconsfield Terraces development in 1890 shows Knapp's house surrounded by what he called "English terrace" apartments. To the right of the Knapp House was the "casino" (clubhouse). Aspinwall Hill is visible in the background. In 1893, Knapp's extensive building program led to financial difficulties. A Beaconsfield Trust was formed as Knapp began to lose financial control. His son Eugene Jr. took over the development of the land west of Tappan Street in 1895, but he later died in a boating accident. (BPL.)

These stone and brick residential blocks were part of Eugene Knapp's Garrison Road property. The block to the right, called "Gordon Terrace," was erected in 1891–92, by Fehmer & Page, architects. The same architects designed the two Georgian Revival blocks, "Bernard Terrace" and "Parkman Terrace," in 1892. Described as an "experiment in domestic economy," the Beaconsfield development was an early condominium arrangement in which people individually owned their own units and shared communal amenities, such as a park, stables, clubhouse, and tennis courts. A central boiler house provided heat for the entire complex. (BPL.)

Knapp located his Beaconsfield development between the new trolley line on Beacon Street and the Boston & Albany Railroad. Behind the railroad station are stables for the residents' horses, designed in 1890 by Fehmer & Page. The stables accommodated 250 horses with a carriage room, harness room, and hay loft. Bells connected the stables to the houses so owners could ring for their horse and carriage. The railroad station was not built until 1906, when Henry Whitney took control of the development. (Courtesy Joel Shield.)

Eugene Knapp was no longer involved in the development and he later committed suicide. By 1903, Henry M. Whitney continued to build new structures, including this "apartment hotel" designed by Fehmer & Page on the site of the casino and part of the park. The hotel had two hundred rooms and a large elegant oval dining room for the residents. It burned in 1966. (Courtesy Tim Sullivan.)

Eight

FISHER HILL

The first houses built on Fisher Hill stood on farmland along the south slope overlooking Boylston Street. Originally the Sherburne Road, this section of Boylston Street later became part of the Worcester Turnpike. During the 18th century, Dr. Zabdiel Boylston, famous for the introduction small pox inoculations in 1721, lived in the house at 617 Boylston Street. Another early house is the one built by Benjamin Goddard in 1810–11, which was moved to its present site on Sumner Road in 1887.

In 1844, the Brookline Reservoir was constructed, providing a picturesque vista from Fisher Hill. This was certainly an important consideration when Henry Lee acquired the Boylston property in 1850. Lee built a brick country home on the site of an older structure. At the same time Francis Fisher, for whom the hill came to be named, also acquired property at the corner of Chestnut Hill Avenue and built a house. A third estate was established by Jacob Pierce on the west side of the hill over-looking Chestnut Hill Avenue.

As late as 1884, there were still only a few houses built on Fisher Hill, mostly on the south slope. Dry goods magnate Joseph H. White built the largest estate on the south side of the hill in 1881–82. The Boston and Albany Railroad circumvented the hill on the north and east, effectively cutting off development from that direction. On the west side Fisher Avenue began at what is now Hyslop Street next to the Pierce estate on Chestnut Hill Avenue and extended up the hill past the covered reservoir established by the town in 1875. White and Pierce were among the landowners who, in 1884, hired Frederick Law Olmsted to prepare a development plan for Fisher Hill along lines that would encourage the construction of large, single-family homes. Much of Fisher Hill is included as part of the Fisher Hill National Register District.

Buckminster was one of the first roads to be completed. Between 1888 and 1892 there were 11 houses built on this road. While these houses were being built, other roads planned by the Olmsted firm were under construction, opening up lots on Leicester, Hyslop, Holland, Clinton, and Dean, as well as an extension of Fisher Avenue north of Buckminster. The City of Boston acquired a large portion of the Fisher Estate for a reservoir on the west side of Fisher Avenue. The reservoir, and its Romanesque pump house, was completed in 1886–87.

In 1903, John and Mary Longyear acquired the last large undeveloped parcel on the hill. They assembled a parcel so large that they absorbed a section of Hyslop Road where it originally extended to Leicester. (Hayden Road is a remnant of that extension.) They constructed their large mansion in 1904–06, and later built several smaller homes for members of the Christian Science Church between Seaver Street and Holland Road.

Fisher Hill was a neighborhood of upper-class houses by the early 1900s, however, a number of property owners were concerned about protecting their investments in the face of the rapid increase in demand for multi-family homes elsewhere in Brookline. Areas, which only a few years before had been dominated by single-family homes, were being demolished for construction of apartment blocks. In 1914, a covenant was entered into by 165 Fisher Hill property owners to protect their holdings against "deterioration through the construction of apartment houses, two-family houses, public garages, stores, and hospitals." This covenant expired in 1940, by which time zoning regulations had been established by the town to restrict high-density residential construction. The hill has primarily retained its residential character, although a school was established along Fisher Avenue, Cardinal Cushing College, which today is used by Newbury College.

The oldest portion of this house is believed to date from the 17th century. It was the home of Dr. Zabdiel Boylston, who introduced inoculation against smallpox in 1721. This was highly controversial at the time, as many believed that disease was the will of God and inoculation was sinful. William Hyslop, a wealthy merchant, was probably responsible for extensive improvements to the house between 1766 and his death in 1796. Henry Lee acquired the house as part of his country estate in 1850. (BPL.)

Built by Benjamin Goddard in 1810–11, this building was originally on Boylston Street opposite the reservoir and moved to its present site on Summer Road in 1887. Goddard was a farmer and his diary records much of daily life in Brookline between 1812 and 1854. Before living on this farm, Benjamin and his brother Nathaniel were successful merchants. Upon his death, Benjamin left the property to his brother's children, whose heirs formed the Goddard Land Company that helped initiate the development of Fisher Hill. (BPL.)

Henry Lee lived on Boylston Street in Brookline from 1850 until his death in 1898. A partner in the banking form of Lee, Higginson & Co., he established his estate in Brookline as a rural retreat. Lee was a strong supporter of the acquisition of parks and open space for Brookline. When plans were proposed to widen Boylston Street and install a trolley line in 1896, Lee provided strenuous opposition. He stated, "I deny that rapid transit is the only or the paramount consideration with settlers in the country, and consequently to be sought at all hazards and sacrifices, and I maintain that it interferes with repose and recreation of mind and body . . . " (BPL.)

Henry Lee's estate included the old Boylston-Hyslop House and this brick dwelling nearby. Lee was related by marriage to the architects of the house, Edward and Eliot Cabot. Correspondence between Henry Lee and Eliot Cabot at the time the house was being built in 1853 indicated it was considered unusual to have a red brick house in the country where the traditional color was white. The house was demolished in the 1930s. (BPL.)

Frances Fisher, for whom Fisher Hill was named, built this house in 1852, at the corner of Boylston and Chestnut Hill Avenue. Calvin Ryder designed it. Fisher was a commission merchant who made his fortune in Virginia flour and tobacco before the Civil War. He died in 1871 and Walter Channing acquired the property for use as his private hospital, the Channing Sanitarium. (BPL.)

Known at the time of his death in 1921 as, "an alienist of international renown," Dr. Walter Channing specialized in psychiatry. He was the first Dean of the Harvard Medical School and helped establish the public baths in Brookline. He worked at several mental institutions in Massachusetts and New York and established a private hospital in Brookline in 1879. His own residence, the only house in Brookline known to be designed by H.H. Richardson, was on the site of the present Channing Street off Chestnut Hill Avenue. (BPL.)

Joseph H. White, owner of a large dry goods store in Boston, was one of the first to construct an estate near the top of the hill. White hired Peabody & Stearns to design his Queen Anne house in 1881–82. The grounds were laid out by the Olmsted firm. White built a large brick house for his daughter on Seaver Street, and his brother Jonathan erected a stone residence on Buckminster Road. (BPL.)

Called a "General Plan for subdivision of properties on Brookline Hill," this was the design of F.L. Olmsted and J.C. Olmsted for Fisher Hill in 1884. As originally conceived, the plan extended from Chestnut Hill Avenue on the west to Cypress Street on the east. The road patterns laid out by the Olmsted firm were essentially carried out, which makes Fisher Hill one of the most intact examples of their subdivision plans in the country. (Courtesy of the National Park Serve, Frederick Law Olmsted National Historic Site.)

Joseph Pierce, whose house can just be seen in the center of the photograph, was one of the first to build houses on speculation on Fisher Hill. William Ralph Emerson designed the two Colonial Revival houses, built in 1885, on Fisher Avenue. The house in the right of the photograph still stands at 195 Fisher Avenue. (BPL.)

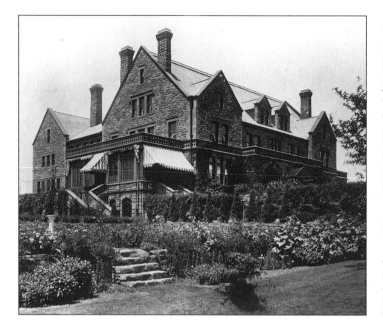

Fisher Hill subdivision was primarily intended for single-family homes on homogeneous-sized lots. John and Mary Longyear departed from that concept in purchasing 8 acres on the top of the hill for their estate. The Longyears dismantled their stone mansion in Marquette, Michigan in 1903, shipped the material to Brookline, and reassembled the house in 1904–06. The architects of both the original house and the reconstruction were Charlton, Gilbert & Kuenzli of Milwaukee, Wisconsin. (SPNEA.)

John and Mary Longyear were students of Christian Science and followers of Mary Baker Eddy. John Longyear earned his fortune primarily in mining and northern Michigan and on the island of Spitzbergen in Norway. Mr. Longyear died in 1921 and his wife passed away in 1931. She created the Longyear Foundation, which included this estate and a collection of historical memorabilia related to Mary Baker Eddy and the First Church of Christ, Scientist she established. (Courtesy of the Longyear Historical Society and Museum.)

The Longyear Mansion was doubled in size as part of the reconstruction on its new site. The grounds were also extensively landscaped by various firms and included a rose garden and swimming pool. To the right, in this c. 1910 photograph, is the sunken garden. The tennis court is on the left. (Courtesy of the Longyear Historical Society and Museum.)

The house pictured above is one of about a dozen constructed on Buckminster in the early stages of the development. J.W. Dunklee of the Goddard Land Company hired Edgar Allen Poe Newcomb to design this house and stable, which cost $18,000. Completed in 1892, the house was purchased by a Boston lawyer, Nathaniel Walker. (Courtesy Lynn Osborn.)

The rapid development of houses on Fisher Hill made it necessary to construct a neighborhood school for the new population. Runkle School was named for John D. Runkle, second president of MIT, and member of the school committee. Erected in 1896, the original school is visible to the right in the photograph. Peabody & Stearns designed two additional structures, creating a U-shaped courtyard in 1901–02. (Courtesy Dan Miranda.)

Nine

COOLIDGE CORNER

Coolidge Corner, the area around Harvard and Beacon Streets, was first developed in 1851, when Beacon Street was laid out as a county road. Previously open land on the road to the college, or Harvard Street, was established in 1662 (named in 1841). Beacon Street was a narrow, country road designed to open north Brookline to development and to provide access to Boston across the Mill Dam, built in 1821, for businessmen who chose to live outside the city. After the county way was put in, a scattering of single-family houses were erected along the route and on the satellite roads, Marion Street, Center Street, and Short Street. Alexander Wadsworth, civil engineer, designed the area around St. Mark's Church with substantial house lots in 1844. All that remains of this development is St. Mark's Square. Where the new road intersected Harvard Street was a logical place to put a general store, a school, the hay scales, and watering trough. In 1854, the Harvard School was built on an island where the Art Deco Bank is located.

After the Civil War, several large homes were built, especially along the southern slope of Corey Hill. Henry Whitney, president of the West End Land Company and Brookline Park Commissioner, consolidated the horse car routes in Boston. Part of his major scheme was the widening of Beacon Street and a new transportation route. He hired Frederick Law Olmsted Sr. and John Olmsted to design plans to widen the road to 200 feet. The Beacon Street project, originally called the "extension of Commonwealth Avenue along Beacon Street," included two bridle paths, one through lane, one pleasure drive, one lane for walking, and streetcar tracks all separated by a row of trees. There was some opposition, but the plans went through with Beacon Street only enlarged to 160 feet. Construction began in April 1887. This opened the area up for major construction of single-family homes, apartment blocks, and town houses. Most of the single-family homes were replaced and more apartment houses and commercial enterprises were built. With the advent of the trolleys down Beacon and Harvard Streets, Coolidge Corner had supplanted Brookline Village as the major commercial area by the turn of the century.

The 1920s saw another burst of construction and defined its present character. Concrete one- and two-story commercial buildings, the Hotel Pelham, and the Durgin garage were built, along with more apartment blocks. Constructed in 1926 along the plans of Arthur H. Bowditch, the Hotel Pelham was the site of the first American home of Arnold Schoenberg, the Viennese composer. Along Harvard Street, one- and two-story commercial blocks were constructed of early cast concrete.

The Coolidge Corner Arcade Building is the most unique structure constructed in 1927. It was made with a cast-stone facade along the designs of G.N. Jacobs. He also designed the Coolidge Corner Building at the corner of Harvard and Beacon. The building, at the corner of Babcock Street, originally constructed in 1921 and remodeled in 1988, was the WW II home of a corps of army counterintelligence agents.

Along with residential and commercial blocks, came institutions molding the character of the area. The religious institutions were the Harvard Street Church (now the United Parish Church), St. Mark's Methodist Church (now a residential condominium), the Baptist church, the Universalist church, the Second Unitarian Church (now Temple Sinai), and Temple Ohabei Shalom.

At the corner of Beacon and Harvard Streets, on the site of the S.S. Pierce building, stood the Italianate storefront of the Coolidge family. The only commercial enterprise in north Brookline for years, it was established in 1857 by David Coolidge with his cousins William & Thomas Griggs. David's brother William ran the store until 1884. The store was the informal headquarters of Democrats in the 19th century and was nicknamed, in the 1860s, as the "Copperhead Crossroads." The area was named on early maps as Coolidge's Corner. (BPL.)

This was the house of General James Whitney, father of Henry Whitney. Located at the corner of Pleasant Street, the house was constructed in 1857 on Stearns's land by Charles Wilder. Wilder sold it to Whitney in 1865. Whitney had been the superintendent of the Springfield Armory under President Buchanan and the president of several steam ship companies. He was also involved in the building of the Back Bay and Fenway area of Boston. He lived here until his death in 1878; his widow lived until 1909. Although spared when Beacon Street was widened, the house gave way to a commercial block in 1912. (BPL.)

Henry L. Whitney was the entrepreneur who conceived and built Beacon Street. He began buying land around Beacon Street as early as the 1870s, and he consolidated the Boston horse car companies. To promote his development, he hired Frederick Law Olmsted to devise a plan for residential development and transit lines. Originally known as the extension of Commonwealth Avenue along Beacon Street, Olmsted and John C. Olmsted proposed a 200-foot avenue with tracks, and walking and riding lanes all separated with four tree lines. Whitney established an electric trolley line into Boston—the West End Railway Company. It is the longest running electric trolley in the country. Its success sparked a nationwide transit boom in the late 19th century. Whitney died in 1923. (BPL.)

Looking north from Beacon Street on Short Street, the house of William Hill, a Boston merchant, was built c. 1860. It was part of the early development of this area of Beacon and Corey Hill, after the construction of the county way in 1851. (BPL.)

This magnificent Queen Anne house, designed by E.A.P. Newcomb, stood on Park Street. This residence was built in 1882 for Daniel W. Russell, a Brookline real estate developer. Russell was engaged in the life insurance business and eventually established an agency of the New York Life Insurance Company in Boston. He also became a local developer, buying property in Brookline as early as 1874. He moved into Brookline in 1880. He developed the area around Cypress and Gorham along with the section around Vernon and Auburn Streets. (BPL.)

Looking east, this area is in transition with an old 18th-century house surrounded by the beginnings of the commercialism of Coolidge Corner. The land and house passed from the Sewall family into the hands of Charles Stearns in 1819, whose holdings stretched all the way to Charles Street. At the entrance stood an elm that had been saved when Beacon Street was built in 1851. By 1904, Stearns had taken advantage of the development, building a wooden, one-story, real estate office, and adding a bank in 1910. The truck is carrying water to reduce the dust from the streets. (Courtesy Joel Shield.)

The George Armstrong house was one of the first structures built after the widening of Beacon Street. In 1887, he hired Shepley, Rutan & Coolidge to design this shingle residence and stable. Soon after its erection, Armstrong hired Frederick Law Olmsted to design the garden. Armstrong was the president of Armstrong Transfer Company and of the Armstrong Dining Room and News Company as well as the director of several railroads. It was sold in 1913 and demolished for the commercial block. (*Engineering Record*, November 1890.)

On the site of the James Whitney House at Pleasant Street in the 1930s, is the Medieval Revival one-story commercial block built in 1912. The commercial Gothic-style Coolidge Corner Building was built the same year. Both buildings were designed by Arthur Bowditch, a Brookline architect who lived on Pill Hill and who designed several major buildings on Beacon Street, such as the Stoneholm building. (BPC.)

This is a view of the Coolidge Corner area in the early 1930s, with ornate and lively one-story commercial blocks. The block on the left shows the decorative swirls of Art Deco while the buildings across are more classical in style, built 1926 with E.B. Stratton as architect. Billboards had already made inroads, as had automobiles. The old Universalist church is visible on the right, just before its transformation into the Coolidge Corner Theatre. (BPC.)

This is a view of the area around Coolidge Corner in 1933, taken from the roof of a commercial block Harvard Street. The S.S. Pierce Building, on the site of the Coolidge Brothers store was designed in 1898 by Winslow & Wetherell for Wallace Pierce, son of the founder. The original store contained Whitney Hall, which was used for dances, meetings, and parties. The Victorian Gothic Harvard Church, now the United Parish Church, was built as a Congregational church in 1871–73, designed by Edward T. Potter. The Queen Anne house at the corner is one of the last remnants of single-family homes that were built around Coolidge Corner c. 1890. (BPC.)

In 1906, the Beacon Universalist Society bought land and constructed this block from designs of C. Howard Walker. In 1933, the Harvard Amusement Company hired Ernest Hayward to convert the building to a movie theater. After many years of contentious debate, Brookline finally had its first moving picture theater, "The Brookline." It opened with a movie on Brookline's history, a Disney short, and "Only Yesterday, Saturday's Millions." Today it is the only operating Art Deco theater in the Boston area. (BPC.)

Here is a view looking east toward Boston and the Stearns house. The buildings on the right, built in the 1890s, were mixed residential and commercial. This photograph shows the original design of Beacon Street with the trolley down the middle, bridle path or grass strip, and the tree lines. The trolley stops were built in 1902, by the Boston Elevated Railway. Originally right across from each other, the outbound one was moved in 1924. (Courtesy Joel Shield.)

This is the same set of buildings from the opposite direction and approximately 15 years later. This view from the 1930s, shows the view from the old Brookline Trust building, built 1919, Thomas James, architect. The Baptist church, designed by Julius Schweinfurth in 1906, stood until 1971. Its bell remains outside the modern building. Notice the paving on Beacon Street and the recent introduction of parking on the bridle path. (BPL.)

This old postcard shows the character of Beacon Street near Amory Playground. Few single-family houses were built in the early years, with the predominant building type being town houses and apartments, usually built in long continuous rows, providing harmony, rhythm, and uniformity to the street. The elm trees were still alive and the carriage lane still intact. (Courtesy Dan Miranda.)

Pictured is the courtyard of Richmond Court, the first Tudor garden apartment building in New England, designed by Ralph Adams Cram in 1898. Lee Lawrie designed the statue fountain. (BPL.)

Gracing the corner of Beacon and Summit Avenue stood the Raymond-Mitton House. It was built in 1862 by E.A. Raymond with a greenhouse and a stable for the resident coachman. It was sold to Mitton in the 1890s. The Mittons enlarged and remodeled the house to the Colonial Revival style, building more greenhouses and more elaborate landscaping. The Mitton family sold the property to the Beacon School in 1917. The house and grounds were demolished in 1925. The short-lived era of large single-family houses was coming to an end. (BPL.)

Here is Summit Avenue in the 1930s. The Raymond-Mitton house has been replaced with the commercial building on the left built in 1925, by Gay & Proctor for Thomas Elcock. The Art Deco block designed on the right was erected in 1926 from the design of F.A. Norcross. Summit Avenue leads to the top of Corey Hill. A newsboy sits with his wagon, waiting for a customer. (BPC.)

96

Ten
WASHINGTON SQUARE AND COREY HILL

Washington Square is the name of the district surrounding the intersection of Beacon and Washington Streets. Washington Street was laid out from Brookline Village in 1657 as the road to Watertown. It was the road taken by cattle going to the Brighton stockyards. It bordered on land belonging to the Cottons, Sharps, Whites, and Griggs and remained unsettled until the late 1700s. In the early 1790s, John Robinson and Enos Withington, from Dorchester, bought 2 acres of swampland near Fairbanks Road and established a tannery along the brook. It remained in their families for years. The Enos Withington House stood next to the old gasometer site. The other early house in this area was built by the Corey family near the town line to Boston. As in Coolidge Corner, the construction in 1851 of Beacon Street had a major impact on the development of this area. The widening in 1887 resulted in the construction of grander houses, apartment blocks, and commercial structures. The open area around Washington and Beacon Streets developed as a streetcar suburb of middle-class housing which remains today. The increased population led to the construction of the Michael Driscoll School in 1911 and the construction of two churches: the Leyden Congregational Church and the All Saint's Church. The Leyden Congregational Church has been the Chinese Christian Church of New England since 1975. The commercial character of the intersection itself reflects the early 20th-century building activity.

This area is framed and dominated by Corey Hill, rising 260 feet above sea level, known in the early settlement period as "The Great Hill." In the 18th century, it was a place of wooded groves, pastures, and working farms. Begun in mid-19th century and spurred by Beacon Street widening, it has become a dense residential area of single- and multifamily structures, apartment buildings, and institutions. Throughout this period, its main distinction has been the extraordinary view. In the early 1760s, it was originally settled by Timothy Corey from Weston, who married Elizabeth Griggs, from another prominent early Brookline family. As late as 1800, Elijah Corey's land was described as having a "natural growth of trees and orchards laden with fruit." Corey also raised dairy cattle and sent a wagon loaded up with milk every day to Faneuil Hall. By 1874, more houses had been built, mostly for merchants. Much of this land was eventually bought by Eben Jordan of Jordan & Marsh. His estate developed and built upon the land sloping towards Washington Street. A portion around Jordan Road was not developed until 1927. The view and air led to the establishment of several hospitals on the hill near the turn of the century.

Summit Avenue was originally laid out in 1868, as a rough path for agriculture purposes. The popularity of sightseers visiting "The Great Hill" led to its improvement; it was paved and a plank walk was put in for pedestrians. President Eliot of Harvard and Louis Agassiz were among the visitors. As many as 400 visitors were recorded on one Sunday. The town bought land at the summit in 1900 and bought another piece across the road in 1915; both are now parks.

Bartlett Farm on Washington Street is at the base of Corey Hill. In 1843, Deacon Corey sold his house and 40 acres up to the top of the hill to James Bartlett for $10,000. Bartlett resided here for 30 years until his death around 1873. The property was sold to Eben Jordan, who established the Jordan Marsh Company in 1850. Jordan bought it for an investment at a reported price of $115,000. It was laid out in lots and slowly sold over time. (BPL.)

Located across from what is now Englewood Avenue, this house was owned by Dr. Simonds in 1874. By 1875, it was listed as the Reservoir Hotel with Andrew Johnson as proprietor. In the 1880s, this establishment was labeled "notorious" in the papers and was continually being shut down for selling liquor. In December 1885, the proprietor, Dr. Simonds, was fined $100 and jailed for aiding in the maintenance of a common nuisance. This complex was torn in 1893. (BPL.)

Standing all alone on upper Beacon Street at the corner of the now Williston Road, the Isaac D. White House was built in 1866. This rear photograph shows the stuccoed Italianate house and its commanding view of Corey Hill to the east. The house was demolished in 1927 and replaced with the one-story block of stores and restaurants. (BPL.)

The corner of Winthrop and Beacon Streets is seen here on the eve of the widening. The photograph shows the rural, undeveloped quality of this section of Beacon Street. The land belonging to Boston University was slowly sold off and developed. (BPL.)

One of the most fanciful houses designed by Obed F. Smith, this house was built atop Corey Hill for Mr. Dwinell, bookkeeper for Amos A. Lawrence. He moved to Corey Hill under his doctor's orders to live on high ground because of ill health. After regaining his health, Dwinell sold the house and barn to George Francis Fabyan, a dry goods and commission merchant in Boston. Fabyan enlarged and improved the property, living here until 1884. He also built several houses on Mason Terrace for an investment. (BPL.)

Architect Alfred S. Bither designed the house of Jerome Jones on Summit Avenue in 1874. Jones was a manufacturer of glass and earthenware in Boston. He also was the vice-president of the Home Savings Bank, and a member of the Boston Merchants Association and the Brookline First Parish Church. When this house was built, there was only one other on the hill. In 1927, it became Bellevue Hospital. A barn was torn down in 1946. In 1976, the hospital moved out and it became office space and has since been converted to five dwelling units. (BPL.)

The intersection of Washington and Beacon Streets and Corey Hill shows the Jordan house, in the center, an apartment row house, built in 1897, and the corner commercial block designed by Ernest Boyden for Charles Merrill in 1898. It contained stores, offices, and a hall for concerts and dances. (BPL.)

Taken c. mid-1890s, Beacon Street is in the immediate years after the widening. The Jordan, Sias, and Chase houses are built, the stairs going up to Corey Hill are in, and the trees are planted. Most of the trees along Beacon Street were elms. Along this section, however, Jacob Pierce gave one hundred red oaks and James Bowditch gave more than 40 pin oaks, which were planted in line with the red oaks. The trolley is going out-bound, while a carriage is going towards Coolidge Corner. (BPL.)

At the corner of Lancaster Terrace sat the expansive shingle house of Caleb Chase, built in 1889, designed by Willard Sears. Chase was co-founder and president of Chase & Sanborn. A flight of pink Braintree granite stairs led up to the house. It had a 15-foot circular verandah. The family rooms on the second floor were decorated in silk; the third floor contained a billiard room with a spectacular view. In 1967, it was torn down. (Courtesy Jenna and Aly Kidrin.)

John Webber, previously of 269 Kent Street, moved to Beacon Street when E.S. Tobey designed this Romanesque structure with its carriage house. After his move to Beacon Street, he engaged extensively in the real estate business. Webber's most elaborate venture was the construction of the Stoneholm, Brookline's magnificent Beaux-Art apartment block. (Courtesy Jenna and Aly Kidrin.)

The house on the right originally stood at 1560 Beacon; it was moved up the hill in 1903. Built by Charles D. Sias, an executive at Chase & Sanborn, in 1889, it was designed by Arthur Vinal. The house on the left belonged to King Gillette, inventor of the safety razor. It was built in 1892 by Ben Lombard and designed by Little, Brown & Moore. Gillette moved here with his family in 1907. It was demolished in 1944. (BPL.)

By 1900, Frederick McQuestern, who worked for the George McQuestern Lumber Company in East Boston, had bought the Sias house. Deciding he wanted a bigger house on Beacon Street, he purchased a lot on Mason Terrace from Henry Whitney, to which he moved the house. He then built the new house shown here, a more conservative Colonial Revival designed by Winslow & Wetherell in 1903. This house was demolished in 1967 for an apartment building. (BPC.)

A panorama showing the upper row of Beacon Street and Corey Hill was taken *c*. 1904. It shows how much had been built since the 1890s photograph. Perhaps one of the most impressive residences to be built on Beacon Street was the stone mansion of Eben Jordan Jr. Stonehurst was designed by Winslow & Wetherell in 1890. Jordan lived here from 1891 to 1898, when he moved to his father's house on Beacon Hill after Jordan Sr.'s death. He also

became president of Jordan Marsh & Co. The house remained vacant until 1905 when Peleg Briggs Wadsworth turned the house into apartments. From about 1920 to 1947, Miss Augusta Choate ran the Choate School here. The mansion was demolished in 1955. (Library of Congress.)

Brandon Hall was built in 1903–04 as an apartment and hotel at 1501 Beacon Street, with A.G. Eastman as the architect. During WW II, it was used as a residence for SPARS, women of the Coast Guard. Right after the war, before the Coast Guard equipment was removed, a great fire took place with six city fire departments responding. The interior was gutted and all that remained were the columns. (Courtesy Dan Miranda.)

The Romanesque two-family town house was constructed at the corner of Winthrop and Beacon Streets for B.C. Hastings, designed by P.W. Ford. The town house form was a popular type during the first decades after the widening of Beacon Street. This site now houses an ice cream store, a bank, and a fruit store. (Courtesy Joel Shield.)

This brick-and-limestone-stepped, gabled fire station was designed by G. Fred Crosby in 1898. When it was finished, the aerial ladder from the village and the Engine #2 from the Devotion Street station were moved here. The huge wooden doors were replaced in 1947. This is the only station that retains its original hose tower. This view shows Dick and his Brownie with two white horses. Brownie retired in 1906 at the age of 15, having served the fire department for 15 years. (BPL.)

The Brookline Gas Company was organized in 1851. It provided gas for the new system of streetlights, erecting 25 in 1853 and maintaining them for $25 a year. Four large gasometers were constructed to store and measure the gas. This structure was the last on this Washington Street site, built in 1872, between the two tanneries. By 1917, it had become a garage and gas station with commercial buildings around it. Before its demolition in 1984, it also served as a disco and a radio station. (BPC.)

This two-family Colonial Revival house built at 33 Bartlett Crescent was typical of the moderate streetcar suburb housing that grew up after the Beacon Street widening. Like most of this part of Corey Hill, it had been part of Eben Jordan landholdings in Brookline. It was sold and developed around the turn of the century. Most of Bartlett Crescent was developed by the Frost Brothers and their architect, J. Merrill Brown, a popular suburban designer in Brookline and Newton. (Courtesy Joel Shield.)

Eleven
CHESTNUT HILL

This section of Brookline was named Chestnut Hill by Francis Lee, who built the first country house in this vicinity during the 1850s. Lee's house was located in the Newton portion of Chestnut Hill and his property extended into Brookline. The original Chestnut Hill community was planned to accommodate family and friends, similar to what Amos Lawrence was doing in Cottage Farm at the same time. All of the first houses were located in Newton, and it was not until the mid-1880s that the Brookline portion of this land began to be intensively developed.

At the same time that several Boston Brahmin families were establishing country homes north of Boylston Street, a large Catholic cemetery was built on the south side of that road. Holyhood Cemetery, laid out in 1857, reflected the mid-19th-century influence of romantic landscape planning by Mt. Auburn Cemetery in Cambridge. The curving roads, landscaped grounds, and rural setting was very much in keeping with the popular notion that cemeteries should also serve the living in terms of providing a park for visitors. Many prominent Catholics are buried here, including Joseph and Rose Kennedy.

In 1888, landscape architect Frederick Law Olmsted was asked to prepare plans for a subdivision for the lands between Reservoir Lane, Boylston Street, and the border with Newton. These plans were never carried out and the land began to be sold off for house lots in the 1890s. Charles Miller, a Boston real estate broker, sold much of the property for large single-family homes. By 1897, there were over two dozen new houses on Norfolk, Devon, Circuit, and Boylston Streets. The Chestnut Hill Golf Club was also established at this time. The course and its small clubhouse were located on what is now Fairway Road north of Boylston Street.

To the south of Boylston Street were several large estates, including those of John G. Wright and William Cox, which are now the Soule Playground and Recreation Center, and Pine Manor College respectively.

Development of Chestnut Hill as a residential neighborhood of large single-family homes continued in the first half of the 20th century. The Chestnut Hill Railroad Station in Newton, as well as Boston & Worcester Trolley Line on Boylston Street, made this area accessible for Boston commuters. In addition to the Chestnut Hill Golf Course, recreational facilities included the Longwood Cricket Club. The clubhouse is in Newton but the famous tennis courts are in Brookline.

The Chestnut Hill Golf Club owned one of the last large undeveloped parcels when it was sold to the Chestnut Hill Corporation in 1933. The land was subdivided into house lots. Notwithstanding the Great Depression, a large number of homes were built in the mid-1930s. House construction continued in the 1940s and 1950s before the old golf course land was fully developed.

A major early landmark on Heath Street near Hammond was the Richards Tavern. The house was built about 1760 by Elhanon Winchester, a follower of the "New Lights," an evangelical revival group which helped him construct the house on condition that services could be held here. Winchester had been a Congregationalist, and he lost interest in the New Lights, converted to Baptist, then to Unitarian, and finally became a Shaker. Ebenezer Richards acquired the property for a tavern as there was a tollgate for the Worcester Turnpike in the rear of the property. (BPL.)

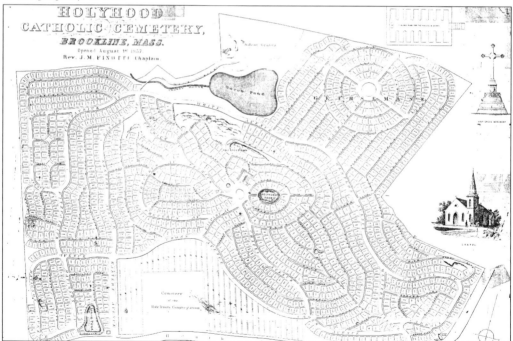

The plans are seen here for Holyhood Cemetery, 1857, designed by Shedd & Edson, civil engineers and surveyors. The plans for this romantic rural cemetery were never entirely carried out. Its location well beyond large population centers of Catholics caused its early development to proceed very slowly. Nonetheless, a number of prominent Catholics are buried here, including the parents of John F. Kennedy and John Boyle O'Reilly, poet and editor of the *Boston Pilot*. (BPC.)

The Boston & Worcester Street Railway opened a line from Newton to Cypress Street in Brookline in 1900. The intersection of Hammond and Boylston Streets, shown here, developed as a small commercial district with neighborhood stores. L.H. Graves' pharmacy, on the southwest corner, was built shortly after the streetcar line was established. (Courtesy Joel Shield.)

Theodore Lyman Jr. was the mayor of Boston in 1834–35 and was famous for having rescued William Lloyd Garrison from an anti-abolitionist mob, and for preventing anti-Catholic riots. He first owned a country estate in Waltham; and it was not until 1842 that he began a new country house on Singletree Hill in Brookline. Completed in 1844, Lyman's house had a major impact on the architecture of the region. It was the first use in the Boston area of the Italianate style for a country home. Richard Upjohn, architect of Trinity Church in New York, provided the designs. It was demolished in 1956. (Courtesy Jenna and Aly Kidrin.)

Theodore Lyman Jr. lived only five years after the completion of his Brookline estate. His son, Theodore III, lived here until his death in 1897. Taught by Louis Agassiz at Harvard, he used his scientific training in public service as a fish commissioner for the State of Massachusetts, running experiments for the cultivation and protection of that important industry. The author of reports and scientific papers, trustee and benefactor of several nonprofit organizations, he also found time to serve in the United State Congress. (BPL.)

As the principal thoroughfare through Brookline, Boylston Street was frequently widened and improved. This section of the road, between Reservoir Road and Chestnut Hill Avenue, was not far from the Lyman Estate. A cluster of multi-family housing was developed here by John O'Hearn and Daniel Duffly at the turn of the century. Just visible in the left of the photograph is the first fire station in this area. It was replaced by the existing structure on the opposite side of the street. (BPL.)

Near the junction of Hammond and Boylston is Dunster Street, where architect Herbert Jaques built a house in 1887. Jaques was a partner in the firm of Andrews, Jaques & Rantoul, which designed many houses in Chestnut Hill. Jaques was also an avid golfer, and no doubt chose a site for his house close to the Chestnut Hill Golf Club. The house underwent a major remodeling in the 1930s, and was recently demolished for the new Longyear Museum. (Courtesy Eleanor Motley Richardson.)

There are similarities in the design of Herbert Jaques's own house and the large estate the firm designed for Mr. and Mrs. William E. Cox. The Cox estate, built between 1889 and 1891 on Heath Street, included stables, barns, and other outbuildings, most of which still survive as part of Pine Manor College. Historically called "Roughwood," the estate was enlarged in the early 1900s by Ernest Dane. Ernest Dane was a Harvard-educated banker who, after acquiring his Brookline estate, retired to his gentleman's farm. He was also active in town affairs, including serving on the Board of Selectmen. (BPL.)

Another prominent architect who lived in Chestnut Hill was Horace Frazer. Frazer designed his own house at the intersection of Heath Street and Boylston Street. Architects Chapman & Frazer, designed more houses in Brookline than any other architects did. In Chestnut Hill alone, the firm was responsible for about two dozen residences between 1890 and 1916. In the same period, they designed at least 67 houses throughout the town as a whole. (Courtesy Earle G. Shettleworth Jr.)

This house on Norfolk Street, an 1896 Tudor dwelling, is very typical of Chapman & Frazer's work. Notwithstanding the large number of upper-middle-class houses by this firm, the architects were able to draw upon a seemingly inexhaustible supply of variations for a given style. The floor plan for these houses typically provided, at a smaller scale, all of the rooms found in a grand mansion, the entrance hall, a library, a reception room, a dining room, and a den. (Courtesy Earle G. Shettleworth Jr.)

Chapman & Frazer were equally successful in obtaining clients who could afford large country estates. John G. Wright, in 1896–97, built his "country house," now the site of the Augustus Soule Playground. The grounds were designed by the Olmsted firm. Wright was a wool merchant who had lived on Walnut Street prior to his acquisition of the Thomas Quimby farm. This photograph of the terrace side of the mansion was made by the Olmsted firm in the summer of 1897 before the completion of their landscape plans. (Courtesy National Park Service, Frederick Law Olmsted National Historic Site.)

The stable for the Wright Estate is about the size of one of Chapman & Frazer's single-family homes in Chestnut Hill. This *c.* 1900 photograph shows the building after the Olmsted landscaping, and conveying the sense of the country estate with a cow grazing in the foreground. The stable is now the headquarters for the Brookline Recreation Department. (Courtesy Earle G. Shettleworth Jr.)

The Rivers School acquired the Wright Estate in 1942 and converted the house for classrooms and offices. The Tudor mansion was ideal for the popular image of a private school, and the grounds of the estate were easily adapted for athletic activities. When the Rivers School moved to Weston the town purchased the property for recreational purposes. The house burned two years later. (Courtesy the Rivers School.)

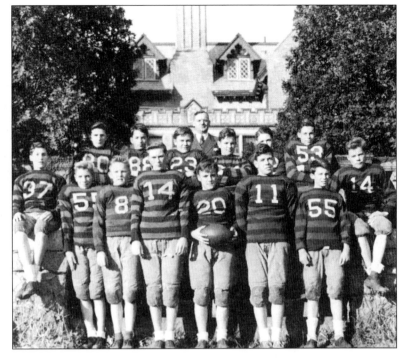

Chestnut Hill had two neighborhood schools, Heath and Baldwin. Heath, the oldest, was the first building having been constructed on Eliot Street in 1902. Baldwin School, built on Heath Street near Hammond, was designed in 1926 by Kilham, Hopkins & Greeley. It included a kindergarten, shown here, three classrooms, and a playroom. (BPL.)

A little known phase in the development of Chestnut Hill was the golf club that was established on the north side of Boylston Street on the site of the appropriately named Fairway Road. The founders of this golf club were not, we can suppose, overly concerned with the usual necessities found in clubhouses. This primitive structure served its purpose until the land was sold for development in 1933. (BPL.)

BEFORE (in oval) AND AFTER SCENES
AT ALL-GAS COLONY

Boston Consolidated Gas Company was involved in the residential development of the Chestnut Hill Golf Club lands during the 1930s. Architect Raymond Stowell prepared plans for "a modern colony of all gas homes," which were built during the Depression on the last large undeveloped parcel in Chestnut Hill. A photograph from a 1938 brochure shows Hilltop and Fairway Roads at the time of the development. (Courtesy Boston Gas Company Collection, John Burns Library, Boston College.)

Twelve

NORTH BROOKLINE

Harvard Street is one of the oldest roads in town, but north Brookline was not developed intensively until the end of the 19th century. Laid out in 1662 as "the road to the colleges" in Cambridge, Harvard Street was cut through farmland. The Devotion House, an 18th-century dwelling still standing on Harvard Street, is a remarkable survivor of the town's agricultural history. As late as the 1880s, this area of Brookline was still largely farmland. Produce from the Griggs and Coolidge farms in north Brookline was delivered to Boston markets. Babcock and Pleasant Streets, which were laid out between Harvard and Brighton Avenue (now Commonwealth Avenue) during the mid-19th century, are evidence of the first efforts to open this area for residential development. Before 1890, however, only a few farmhouses were erected on these new roads.

The year 1886 was seminal in the development of north Brookline as it was then that plans were accepted for the widening of Beacon Street and the construction of an electric trolley line from Boston to Brighton, via Beacon and Harvard Streets. Shortly afterwards, plans were also developed to build Commonwealth Avenue. With the construction of two grand boulevards and a trolley line running up Harvard Street it was not long before the farmland would be subdivided for building lots.

The single most important developer of north Brookline was David McKay. McKay acquired a large parcel from David Coolidge in 1889. Additional land was acquired in 1894 and 1895 and McKay became the principal developer of this neighborhood. Coolidge, Thorndike, Fuller, Clarence, Naples, and Gibbs all contain a large number of homes built by McKay. Peter Graffam was another significant developer, constructing houses on Naples, Osborne, Abbottsford, and Manchester.

Original owners of houses worked in managerial positions that required a daily commute to Boston. Salesmen, physicians, ministers, and owners of small businesses also acquired or built homes in this neighborhood. Several different architectural firms were hired in order to obtain a greater variety in the appearance of the houses. Charles E. Park, Samuel J. Brown, Rand & Taylor, and Greenleaf & Cobb were firms that specialized in suburban design and were responsible for most of the houses built in the McKay and Graffam developments during the 1890s.

During the early 20th century, the growing demand for housing led to the construction of less expensive homes and apartment blocks, such as those on Beals Street where the Kennedy family first moved in 1914. In order to serve the growing population, stores were built on both sides of Harvard Street, often displacing homes less than 30 years old. Gas stations were also constructed as more commuters began to rely on the automobile for transportation. At the same time, north Brookline became the center of a large Jewish community. In 1922–23, a large house of worship was built on Harvard Street—Congregation Kehillath Israel. Ethnic diversity is still present in north Brookline today, where the concentration of shops is known as "JFK Crossing," after the Kennedy birthplace, on Beals Street.

This is a detail of the view from Corey Hill, 1865, drawn by F. Richardson. Looking toward Boston, this representation shows the farms and scattered residences along Harvard Street prior to any significant development of the area. In the left of the view is Babcock Pond and Babcock Hill (covered with trees). (BPC.)

The Devotion House is shown here *c.* 1895. The house built by Edward Devotion in the 17th century was substantially remodeled into its present appearance around the middle of the 18th century. In this photograph parts of the barns are still standing. The picket fence marks the boundary of the first Devotion School building, completed in 1892. The Brookline Historical Society has been responsible for the administration of this historic house since 1911. (SPNEA.)

Babcock Hill and Babcock Pond were eliminated in the course of developing housing lots in north Brookline. This c. 1895 view shows the pond and the hill on the right and Corey Hill in the distance. To the left of the pond is the rear of a house, still standing on Devotion Street, which was built in 1894. Behind it is the tower of the old fire station. (BPL.)

Due to the fast-growing population of north Brookline, a second Devotion schoolhouse was built in 1898, only six years after the first one. Both were designed by Loring & Phipps to occupy lots on either side of the Devotion House, which was threatened with removal. In 1900, the town made a financial commitment toward the preservation of the house and restoration began. (Courtesy Tim Sullivan.)

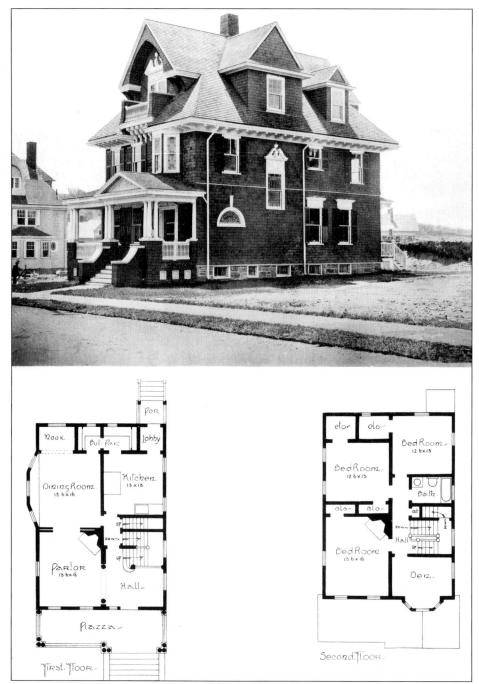

David McKay was a contractor by trade. He hired architects to provide a variety of designs for the exteriors of his houses, but often planned the interiors himself. In this case, the house at 88 Thorndike Street was designed by John H. Hasty. Built in 1895, it was purchased by Frank Waterbury, whose firm of McKenney and Waterbury sold lamps and gas fixtures on Congress Street in Boston. This engraving appeared in the *Scientific American Architects and Builders Edition* in 1897. (Courtesy Earle G. Shettleworth Jr.)

Pictured above is Columbia Street, *c*. 1910, looking toward Corey Hill. Henry Coolidge, who had inherited the family farm, developed most of the houses shown here. He hired a local architect, Alonzo D. Wright, to design his houses, including his own residence, visible in the right of the photograph. (Courtesy Joel Shield.)

Houses built in north Brookline during the 1890s were generally substantial middle-class dwellings with distinctive architectural ornamentation both in the interior and on the exterior. This Babcock Street house was built for John Proctor, a contractor, in 1899–1900 and designed by T. Edward Sheehan. This $14,000 house was on the upper end of the scale for this neighborhood and originally included a stable which was replaced by a large, stylish, automobile garage in 1912. (BPC.)

One of the many young businessmen who purchased homes in north Brookline was Joseph P. Kennedy. The first Kennedy House was on Beals Street, now the John F. Kennedy Birthplace. In 1921, the growing family purchased this house on the corner of Abbottsford and Naples. One of the original houses in the Graffam Development, this house was built by Peter Graffam and sold to Frederick Lovejoy, who worked in Boston in the iron and steel business. Greenleaf & Cobb designed this house in 1897. (Courtesy of John F. Kennedy Library.)

John F. Kennedy is in his Halloween costume, about age nine, in the rear of his Abbottsford Road home. The Kennedy family lived here from 1921 to 1927. Robert F. Kennedy was born here, as were Eunice and Patricia. (Courtesy of John F. Kennedy Library.)

Pictured above is Harvard Street in 1934. By this time, the single-family homes on Harvard Street had been almost entirely replaced by stores and apartment blocks. Kehillath Israel Synagogue is visible on the right. (BPC.)

The Jewish population of Brookline grew significantly in the early 1900s, reaching 4,000 by 1921. Kehillath Israel was constructed between 1922 and 1924, MacNaughton & Robinson, architects, and was the one of the first major synagogues built in town. A school and community building was added in 1928, visible on the right in this 1934 photograph. (Courtesy Kehillath Israel.)

During the 1920s, garages for the storage and service of automobiles were built all along Harvard Street. This garage, erected in 1921, opposite Verndale Street, was designed by Henry F. Bryant, a local architect and engineer. The rather elaborate ornamentation on the building was derived from Federal architecture. This was the period when mechanics and attendants wore uniforms. The automobile garages were similarly "dressed up." (BPC.)

Commonwealth Avenue in Brookline developed along the same lines as the opposite end of the street in Boston. Beginning just before WW I, it became the location for a large number of automobile-related businesses. Typically, these buildings would have richly embellished architectural showrooms on the front and plain concrete garages on the rear. This building was designed in 1924 by Brookline's architect and engineer, Henry F. Bryant. (BPC.)

Beacon Street, at Marion Street in Coolidge Corner, is seen here *c.* 1880. This photograph was taken just before the transformation of Beacon Street into a major boulevard with a trolley line. (BPL.)